DR. EARL HENSLIN

Foreword by Dr. Daniel G. Amen

THIS IS YOUR BRAIN IN L♥VE

New Scientific Breakth... ...gns for a

More Passionate and

Emotionally Healthy Marriage

THIS IS YOUR
BRAIN IN LOVE

OTHER BOOKS BY DR. EARL HENSLIN

This Is Your Brain on Joy

Your Father's Daughter

Man to Man

Forgiven and Free

Off the Cliff: 10 Principles of Business Success

Intervention: Seven Life-Saving Steps

BOOKS COAUTHORED BY DR. HENSLIN

Secrets of Your Family Tree

Inside a Cutter's Mind

THIS IS YOUR
BRAIN IN LOVE

New Scientific Breakthroughs for a
More Passionate and Emotionally Healthy Marriage

Dr. Earl Henslin

with Becky Johnson

THOMAS NELSON
Since 1798

NASHVILLE   DALLAS   MEXICO CITY   RIO DE JANEIRO   BEIJING

Published in Nashville, Tennessee, by Thomas Nelson. Thomas Nelson is a registered trademark of Thomas Nelson, Inc.

Published in association with the literary agency of WordServe Literary Group, Ltd., 10152 Knoll Circle, Highlands Ranch, CO 80130, www.wordserveliterary.com.

Thomas Nelson, Inc. titles may be purchased in bulk for educational, business, fund-raising, or sales promotional use. For information, please e-mail SpecialMarkets@ThomasNelson.com.

Unless otherwise noted, Scripture quotations are taken from the New King James Version®. © 1982 by Thomas Nelson, Inc. Used by permission. All rights reserved.

Scripture quotations marked NIV are from the Holy Bible, New International Version®. © 1973, 1978, 1984 by International Bible Society. Used by permission of Zondervan. All rights reserved.

Scripture quotations marked MSG are taken from *The Message* by Eugene H. Peterson, © 1993, 1994, 1995, 1996, 2000. Used by permission of NavPress Publishing Group.

Scripture quotations marked NLT are taken from the Holy Bible, New Living Translation, © 1996. Used by permission of Tyndale House Publishers, Inc., Wheaton, Illinois 60189. All rights reserved.

Library of Congress Cataloging-in-Publication Data

Henslin, Earl R.
  This is your brain in love : new scientific breakthroughs for a more passionate and emotionally healthy marriage / Earl Henslin ; with Becky Johnson.
      p. cm.
  Includes bibliographical references and index.
  ISBN 978-0-7852-2875-2 (pbk.)
  1. Marriage—Religious aspects—Christianity. 2. Love—Physiological aspects. 3. Brain—Religious aspects—Christianity. I. Johnson, Becky Freeman, 1959– II. Title.
  BV835.H457 2009
  248.8'44—dc22

2009032885

Printed in the United States of America
09 10 11 12 13 RRD 6 5 4 3 2 1

I dedicate this book to Benjamin and Grace Henslin,
Rachel and Keith Hengerle, and Amy and Jill Henslin
(and your future husbands). I ask your forgiveness for the times where
I have failed to be the best example as a father and husband. May you
take any wounds and grow through them to a deeper intimacy with your
spouses and God. May you find great joy and fun in the journey as you
deepen in loving and learning together with your spouses throughout life!

Love,
Dad

Happy marriages begin when we marry the ones we love,
and they blossom when we love the ones we marry.
—TOM MULLEN

CONTENTS

ACKNOWLEDGMENTS

Daniel Amen, MD, has been a constant source of encouragement and support in this project. His friendship and willingness to spend time sharing and talking about the application of neuroscience to relationships for more than a decade has been key to this project. Daniel, thank you so much for the gift of your friendship, time, and your heart! David Jarvis, PhD; Daniel McQuoid, PsyD; and Martha Schuyler, PsyD, are the core of Henslin and Associates. Thank you for your insights and contributions during the weekly staff meetings as we have learned about the importance of optimizing brain function for each of our patients and their families.

Vance Shepperson, PhD, and David Koehn, I cherish the years of friendship and support through the good and difficult times of life.

I want to thank Becky Johnson for her gifted insights, artistry in making me sound better than I deserve, and her heartfelt passion for this work. Thank you for your commitment and many hours of work . . . without your help this book would not have made it into print. Thanks to her husband, Greg Johnson, my agent, without whose amazing ability as an agent, this book, along with *This Is Your Brain on Joy,* would never have materialized and blessed so many readers. I also want to thank Laura Kendall and Debbie Wickwire of Thomas Nelson, whose personal involvement and interest have made this book a success.

I also want to thank my friend and physician, Samuel Doolittle, MD; his wife, Judy; and their nurse, Sarah, for their constant encouragement and interest in this project.

Thanks to Pam Inman, my office manager at Henslin and Associates, for working so hard to manage the practice, giving me the time needed to make this book happen.

Most important are the couples who have been a part of the tens of thousands of clinical hours over three decades of daily clinical work, who have taken risks to grow into all God created them to be—spiritually, emotionally, and sexually. May God continue to bless and guide you, always.

In Gratitude for and Memory of
Laura Kendall, Editor, Thomas Nelson Publishers

One bright May morning in 2009, I received an e-mail from Laura Kendall, who had just been assigned by Debbie Wickwire—to my great delight—to edit this book for Dr. Henslin and me. I've known Laura for years, and her reputation for making good books "shine" is known far and wide. At the end of a long project, every writer gets weary, and when Laura wrote, "I'm thoroughly *loving* working on this book!" I wanted to fly to Nashville and hug her.

Now I wish I had done it.

During the editing process, Laura was in much pain with a then undiagnosed illness, yet she never lost her sense of humor and determination to make this book the best it could possibly be. As we worked, we shared lots of mutual encouragement and laughs, making what can be a grueling process fun. Laura passed away on September 2, 2009, after a short bout in the hospital, complications of pneumonia.

I received the final pages of this manuscript the next sunny morning and must admit many of them are tear-stained as I reread our work, remembering this passage and that where Laura had commented, made a joke, or pushed us to be more clear. I feel so privileged that one of the last books Laura edited is the one you now hold. The unseen hand on every good book is the quiet work of a talented editor, making our words and concepts better than they were. And so we want to honor Laura Kendall, her life, and the skill she so sacrificially gave to us and to this project.

—Becky Johnson

The symbol for love is a heart.

"I love you with all my heart."

"I give my heart to you."

"My heart *aches* when you are gone."

How silly, because most love really happens in the Jell-O–like mass of tissue *between your ears*.

But it just doesn't sound very romantic to say:

"I love you with all my brain."

"I give my brain to you." . . . That sounds like a weird science experiment.

Or, "My brain aches when you are gone."

It is your brain that is the organ of loving, learning, and behaving, and as such, at about three pounds, your brain is the largest sex organ in your body. And in this case, *size* really does matter.

As a fellow traveler along the journey of applying brain science to help individuals and families, Dr. Earl Henslin has been a mentor to me, as well as a student and colleague. Throughout the pages of this book, you will find a common theme: evaluating and improving your brain helps to improve your love life.

One of the most fascinating things I have learned from looking at more than 50,000 brain scans is that when you improve how your brain functions, even if it is troubled, you become more thoughtful, more loving, and more effective in all of your relationships. When our brains are troubled, we tend to be angry, inattentive, moody, and unreliable—all things that undermine relationships. When our brains work right, we tend to be thoughtful, loving, consistent, and reliable—all necessary ingredients for great relationships.

Sounds simple, but very few people understand this! In fact, most marital therapy training programs teach students little to nothing about the brain. How crazy is that?

If you are having trouble in your relationships, you need to think about the brain. Undetected brain problems sabotage your ability to relate to and love others. This is true in all types of relationships, such as between lovers, parents and children, employers and employees, and friends.

Issues such as ADD, anxiety, depression, obsessive tendencies, brain trauma, toxic exposure, and even early Alzheimer's disease all unknowingly, seriously sabotage your relationships.

This wise book will help you understand the brain as it applies to love and show you ways to enhance the love in your life and all you do. I am honored to recommend it to you.

—Daniel G. Amen, MD
Author of *Change Your Brain, Change Your Life*

CHAPTER ONE

This Is Your Brain in Love . . . or Is It on Drugs?

The brain in romantic love resembles a huge geological and meteorological event: earthquakes, cyclones, tsunamis.

—JOHN COMWELL, *SUNDAY TIMES ONLINE*

We'd been platonic friends for five years. I had admired his creative leadership in our advertising company, along with his reputation for fairness and kindness," Annie explained.

"I admired her artistic abilities and her winsome smile and wit," David said, squeezing his wife's hand. "Of course I noticed her other obvious assets, but I never pondered them. In truth, I was grieving the loss of my first wife to breast cancer, and it took all my focus just to get through the day for a long time." The couple often talked by phone and e-mail, usually about a project, and saw each other only a few times a year. David worked in New York, and Annie worked out of her home in California.

"Looking back, as the years passed," David says now, "I think a certain tenderness grew between us. Annie seemed to understand the grief I was walking through, and I felt protective of her in a big-brotherly way, since I was several years older. We were fond of each other in the way of compassionate friends."

And that's as far as it went. A friendship of mutual admiration. Professional colleagues. Then one day, in basically one moment, that friendship was set on fire.

As a Christian therapist who uses brain imaging as part of my regular practice, I know that in the Playbook of Love, this sort of friendship-set-on-fire passion can be the most potent and sometimes the most lasting. That is why I asked Dave and Annie if they'd share their falling-in-love story for us in this book. They eagerly agreed, saying, "That's one of our favorite subjects!"

Annie dove right in. "My husband of twenty-something years walked out of our marriage during his apparent midlife crisis. This shocked my entire system to the core. I was stumbling along trying to remember who I was, groping for what was real, and in such agony of heartbreak, it seemed I'd never stop crying and grieving.

"Enter David, kindhearted friend, voice full of compassion. Steady, faithful, good ol' Dave. Having survived the loss of love, he became a rock in the storm, an understanding friend through the minefields of my own brand of grief. But I'd never considered David anything other than a dear friend.

"I was on a business trip and ended up on the shores of Toronto, eating alone at the hotel's restaurant, which happened to be a romantic Italian eatery. Couples all around me were holding hands and peering into each other's eyes or laughing in the familiar way of longtime lovers. I swallowed the lumps rising in my throat, willing myself not to cry. I looked out the window, hoping for a different view, but as fate would have it, couple after couple was strolling hand in hand along Lake Ontario. I reached for my second (or was it third?) glass of Merlot when I heard Dean Martin's recorded voice crooning, 'When the moon hits your eye like a big pizza pie . . . that's amore!'

"That did it. I quickly downed the glass of wine, skipped dinner, and asked for my check. I made my way to my hotel room, threw myself across the bed, reached for my laptop, and sent an e-mail to my friend Dave. As if my heart had taken over my head, I found myself typing, 'If I marry again, David, I hope it is to a man exactly like you.' Whether it was the wine, the vulnerability of my drifting alone in a sea of couples, or a sudden true revelation of the heart, I found myself typing. 'You know what, Dave? I just realized that I think . . . I love you.' I later read that C. S. Lewis, in speaking of his own longtime friendship with and ultimate marriage to Joy Davidson, wrote, 'No one can mark the exact moment at which friendship becomes love.' But for me, at least, the moment when my feelings for David turned to love is crystal clear.

"I pressed *Send* and held my breath, feeling like Meg Ryan in the movie *You've Got Mail*, knowing that with the typing of a few letters, I'd just risked the possibility of another painful rejection."

LOVE ARRIVES; LOGIC TAKES A VACATION

Annie swallowed a sip of tea and continued. "Within minutes, David responded as always, with kindness and candor. He was flattered—said he would pray for me to find a good man sooner rather than later. He was so terribly sorry about the deep pain I was in, as he'd been through a similar agony of soul. But he assumed my grief had left me seeing him through rose-colored glasses. 'You should know I'm not perfect, that I have flaws, that I'm not the Knight in Shining Armor you may imagine.' He wrote, 'Though I think I'd have been a lot better man to you than your sorry ex-husband was, I do not think you are able to be very rational right now. This is a vulnerable time for you.'

"Ouch. My wine-induced confession had been nicely sealed up and tied in a bow by David's sane and benevolent reply, and that should have been the end of that. Back to logic and reason—and to being good ol' platonic friends. But as Blaise Pascal once wrote, 'The heart has its reasons, of which reason knows nothing,' and once the hint of attraction was let out of Pandora's box, we were both suddenly hit with a love potion so great that it took over our senses for the better part of the next year."

"We seemed the least likely of candidates for such a passionate and sudden romance," Dave shared. "Both of us were the middle-aged steady types. Our artsy, more roller-coastering friends would often turn to us as the pillars of stability. I loved my first wife deeply, but our marriage had been less than passionate. Even before her cancer, we were more like close friends and parenting partners than red-hot lovers."

"Though David initially brushed off my confession of love—which really broke all the rules of a normal dating game—our e-mails took on greater frequency and intensity, becoming increasingly flirtatious," Annie said. "Finally, Dave called me one evening after office hours, our first ever nonbusiness phone conversation. I was chatting on and on, and around and around, nervous as could be, and Dave was saying . . . nothing. Finally I asked, 'Are you there?' and he answered, 'I am.' Long pause. 'I was just thinking how much I love listening to the sound of your voice.' I remembered immediately replying, 'Uh-oh . . .' and knowing we'd now officially gone past the point of no return. We would not be 'just friends' any longer. By the end of an hour-long heart-to-heart talk, we agreed to meet for a face-to-face date in Chicago."

Dave picks up the story. "I got off of that airplane and, walking down those long corridors to the baggage claim, all I could think of was holding her, kissing her. So strange to have this sudden unbridled desire after so many years of putting those emotions on hold. There's a Sinatra song 'Oh, Look at Me Now!' that describes a guy who didn't care much about love and diamond rings and all that mushy stuff. But love, it turns out, has a few surprises up its sleeve, and he finds there's a Casanova lover in him after all. That song could have been written for me."

Annie sighs, smiles, and then interrupts. "I, on the other hand, was think-ing that maybe we'd greet each other with a nice side hug, go out to dinner, have some wine, listen to music, maybe dance, hold hands, take it slow . . . maybe a kiss would come at the end of the date."

David winked at her. "But when I saw her in the flesh, and she saw me, it was like a dream. We were under the influence of a force more powerful than logic—two people with pent-up longings now suddenly free to feel again. There was no time to waste. We walked into each others' arms as if we'd belonged there always; our first kiss would have made Romeo and Juliet blush. Or at least, this is the way it felt to us. Does everyone who falls in love, think theirs is the grandest, deepest, and most passionate ever? That no one could have ever loved this way before or after us?"

Annie nodded. "From that first embrace, I was a goner. Every love song on the radio seemed written for me. The flowers in bloom looked like works of art that I'd never noticed before. I could not think two consecutive thoughts without a thought of David popping up between them. I struggled to work, to think, to communicate normally, without breaking into big, silly grins. My body might have been physically present in one situation, but my mind was gone—wrapped up in thoughts and feelings of being with my Love."

David smiled. "I tried to sleep, but every night visions of Annie would interrupt and keep me awake with longing to hold her."

"I could just be thinking of him and my body would respond as if he really were right there with me," Annie confessed. "I was a walking, grinning, sensual being, and every part of my heart that had been in such pain was now flooded with euphoric waves of love and desire. I know that Dave was, in part, my morphine for the aftermath of divorce, which is why counselors often suggest people wait a year after their divorce to date again. There was an addictive and pain-numbing, even crazy aspect to our romance. I once flew through a snow-storm, and on another occasion drove twelve hours to see Dave for six hours, then turned around and drove back."

Dave chimed in, "I was eighteen again. I never dreamed, at almost age fifty, a man could feel like this. I was walking on air and could not stop smil-ing. Is there anything better in life than loving someone and being loved back? I literally felt I was coming alive again. Waking up each morning and knowing that someone on this planet was thinking of me, as I was thinking of her, was beyond euphoric. I asked Annie to marry me as soon as I could, and she said yes before I got the question out!"

"That whirlwind romance started ten years ago, and we're still pretty much ridiculously in love," Annie added. "Sometimes we even get comments from strangers about how much in love we look and how refreshing it is to see. Of course, they probably assume, from our ages, that we've been married for decades!"

LOGIC COMES BACK FROM VACATION

"Not long after we married," Dave said, "I came out of a fog and for the first time felt I could see and think clearly. I realized I'd been in low-grade, long-term depression for at least five years. Then there was that long valley of grief. And when I fell for Annie, I was in that dizzy, love-drugged state of altered consciousness for another eighteen months or so, and suddenly it was like the song says: 'I can see clearly now the rain has gone.' The crazy-addictive type of love began to fade, but what remains is even better. It's what all the poets and musicians and romantics sing about. It's true love."

Annie reached for Dave's hand. "We created our own marketing-graphics company, then moved to a cottage on a beautiful vineyard in Napa Valley, where our adult kids and grandkids often come to visit. We have the most wonderful picnics right in our own backyard, complete with grape juice and pinot noir from our home-grown grapes. We're involved in a ministry of helping to comfort the brokenhearted during life crises and transitions. But most important of all, we flirt like teens and still have a hard time keeping our hands off each other."

As we continued talking, David told me that his parents had been married sixty years and were still crazy about each other, romantic and funny and flirty and touchy. "So I had great marriage mentors," he said. "And I've seen firsthand how a healthy love and healthy body seem to go hand in hand."

DISSECTING PASSION

How many married couples do you know who still radiate with the passion they felt for each other on their wedding day? It is a rare and glorious sight . . . especially in my business.

As a student of the brain, I know that what happened to David and Annie as their friendship was set on fire really was very much like a "mental kidnapping," with their limbic system (the mood center) overtaking their prefrontal cortex (the seat of logic). I know, I know. I sound like such a killjoy, evaluating the mysteries of love as if it could all be dissected and explained on a chart. So here's my disclaimer: Neurotherapists and brain researchers are only barely tapping into a few of the mysteries of what makes two people fall in love and stay in love. And no matter how much we science-types know about brain chemistry and emotions, we're all just as susceptible to the mysterious, tsunamilike forces of love and romantic attraction as the next guy. But humor me a moment. When two brains are hijacked by romantic attraction, they really are under the influence of chemicals as powerful as any street drug.

Once the "love potion" wore off, Annie and David, thankfully, found that the elements for long-lasting love were still there. This is why long-term friends who fall in love tend to have steadier, happier marriages. There was substance and enjoyable camaraderie to their relationship before the love potion hit and drugged their brains silly. Sadly, many a man and woman—

married or simply dating—who don't have a long history of friendship wake from the love fog and realize, sometimes too late, that their passionate romance didn't automatically translate into the kind of love needed for a long, happy life together. When most of us said our vows at the altar of marriage, we hoped to experience the bright flame of passion, often and always, within the comfort and sanctity of marriage. By the number of couples in marital pain staggering into my office each week, I know those high hopes are too often dashed.

With the divorce rate sky-high, and the rate of the intact-but-unhappy marriages even higher, is lifelong passion a pipe dream? Is it possible to find and keep "true love" alive? Can monogamy stay hot? Yes, yes, yes, I am happy to say. At least, for the "blessed few," a term used by marriage and sex therapist Dr. David Schnarch, whose books on sexuality and spirituality have wonderfully influenced the way I counsel couples. Tragically, only about 8 to 15 percent of couples know this kind of love and keep their passion burning until death parts their lifelong embrace. And you'll read more about couples like this, still in their first marriages, who manage to keep the home fires burning for five or more decades. I write this book with hope of helping increase the blessed few to a blessed majority! For couples who are willing to learn the secrets of proactive passion and apply them to their marriage, a close union will be the greatest source of ongoing pleasure for life.

LOVE-DRUNK BRAINS

The brain is a magnificent organ; it starts from the moment you're born and doesn't stop until you fall in love.
—Pat Love, *When the Object of My Affection Is Your Reflection*

What does a brain in the throes of initial romantic passion look like, feel like, behave like? The briefest explanation is that it looks eerily similar to a brain on cocaine. In the following scan, it would be very hard for me or a neurologist to tell if this person were in love or on cocaine—since a brain in either condition would light up like a tipsy Christmas tree. Humans are literally "high on love" when we first get hit with the drugs of love.

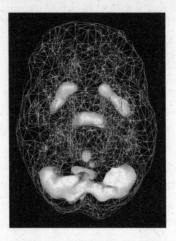

Brain in love or on drugs? Hard to tell!

Two researchers, British brain mapper Semir Zeki and American anthropologist-psychologist Helen Fisher, used brain imaging to explore what happens to brains in the first months of romantic passion. What lit up (on the image above, this looks like eyes and a nose) was the deep limbic system and basal ganglia area, where Helen Fisher concluded that "the chemical storms, leading to infatuation, almost certainly have their physical origin." In romantic love, "the music of cortical sweet reason is drowned out by the primitive drumbeats of our limbic and reptilian brains." Dopamine is among the strongest neurochemicals associated with a feeling of extra energy and heightened awareness singularly focused on the object of desire.[1] As these powerful chemicals (the "love potion") run amok in our brains, they do something very interesting—something that explains why love can make even PhDs seem dopey and wise people do remarkably crazy things. These love chemicals not only produce a natural high, but they also dilute and cancel out the nerve chemical called serotonin. Serotonin, besides having well-known anti-depressant effects, also has anti-obsessive, calming influences on the brain. Healthy doses of serotonin in the brain tend to help us control impulses, unruly passions, and obsessive behavior. It aids the sense of power and logic over our irrational impulses and gives us the feeling of being in control. A severe depletion of serotonin, along with a sharp rise in dopamine, can induce all those classical symptoms that go with the first waves of romantic attraction: panic, anxiety, queasiness, manic behavior, depression, and obsession. This is why people say, "I can't get her or him out of my mind. I'm thinking about this person all the time. I'm obsessed!"

There have even been semi-serious suggestions among scientists that the unhealthily love-obsessed should be given a good dose of an SSRI (anti-obsessive antidepressant) to clear up the brain fog and open their eyes to reality.

Once a couple experiences romantic touching, kissing, and ultimately lovemaking, there is a second chemical storm that takes place deep inside both of their brains. A blast of oxytocin explodes and showers the brain with natural opiates that we know as endorphins, so that new love mimics a "cocaine-on-the-brain" state of mind. A man's oxytocin levels are five times as strong during lovemaking. In women, the oxytocin levels can soar even higher.

Oxytocin, moreover, combines with the hormone vasopressin, which helps create vivid emotional, sensory memories, which in turn deepens feelings for the love object. This little bonding hormone instantly works like superglue to the heart and makes you feel happy, even euphoric, when you hear a piece of music you both love, smell his aftershave, or hear the soft sound of her voice. It makes you prefer the shape, sound, smell, and look of your mate above all others. In several animal studies, scientists have successfully made faithful spouse-snuggling monogamists out of former playboy rodents by giving them doses of vasopressin. And even more interesting, new studies have shown that men who have more vasopressin in their systems tend to make more contented husbands. Maybe someday there will be a test for single girls to give to their potential suitors—to make sure they've got plenty of this "monogamy hormone" in their systems.

These oxytocin highs, with their consequent endorphin hits, do much to explain why it feels like a withdrawal from drugs when the object of our affection goes cold, or worse, is imagined in the arms of another. It is no small wonder that a heartbroken lover's brain is similar to a brain in acute depression. Just as there are serotonin receptors in the brain, there are serotonin receptors in the heart. The literal pain you feel in your heart when you lose someone close to you is the result of these changes in serotonin.

But what happens as time marches on and the neuro-storms that we once expected to light passion's fire begin to diminish? Again, it is similar to the way a body adjusts to a drug that at first produces a euphoric high, but eventually wears off and is less and less effective. Typically, as previously noted, we get the love-chemical cocktail for about six to eighteen months delivered free of charge, service of the Creator. (I've always thought that premarital counseling during this time of intoxication is wasted money and time. When engaged couples come in, I sometimes jokingly suggest they come back to see me in six months, when their brains are detoxed from the love high.) Then the cocktail begins to wear off as the part of the brain that is logical and reasonable comes back into the forefront of our emotional lives. This is where two lovers meet the crossroads of their life together and face three choices:

1. Let go of this relationship and start a new one so you can reexperience the endorphin highs. Then do the same thing again and again and again.
2. Settle for less. Learn to be satisfied with a less than regularly passionate marriage and put your heart into other things, such as your children, work, a hobby, friends, or a new dream.
3. Become Master-Level Lovers—lovers who know the secret of proactive passion and practice it daily for the rest of their married lives. Become the blessed few.

We've all known people—and perhaps you are one—who have chosen the options behind Door 1 and Door 2. Hopefully those of you reading this book would like a peek behind Door 3 and the secrets it holds for a lifetime of passion and love.

If so, turn the page, and we'll start the process of getting a PhD in true, lasting love.

CHAPTER TWO

Sexuality and Spirituality: Divine Balm for Your Soul and Brain

Eroticism is . . . where a man experiences a woman with all his senses and not just his eyes. It's the insatiable desire to know someone completely.

—RABBI SHMULEY

You are never too old to refuel and energize your life or raise your happiness with the chemicals of love—whether you are just falling in love or whether you are holding hands near life's exit ramp. In fact, one of the sweetest loves I ever observed was between a man and a woman who were both looking forward to their one-hundredth birthdays.

I was just a sophomore in college when I began working as an orderly in a nursing home, my first job in the healthcare profession. I was the *only* male in Mankato, Minnesota, working in a nursing home. I can't even remember how I got a job there, but in hindsight I look back on it as a wonderful privilege. Even then, as a young man, I thought it was an incredible experience to work with the elderly and attend to their needs at an age when they could no longer do so many things for themselves.

In the home was one couple I'll never forget: Henry and Martha. I think they were the only married couple in the nursing home at that time. He was ninety-eight, and she was ninety-six. They had been married for more than sixty years. And this was the second marriage! Henry would wait (from what I learned from the other nurses and the other staff) for the day I would be working. I worked the three to eleven shift, and as the clock inched closer to eleven o'clock, Henry would buzz the nurses' station, and

I would go down to his room. Henry always wanted the same thing: for me to help him from his bed over to his wife's bed. I think he was embarrassed to let one of the female nurses or aides help him into his wife's bed. But since I was a guy, it felt okay for him to ask for my assistance. (He'd worked out a similar deal with the morning janitor to move him back to his bed the next morning.)

Now Martha was mostly blind, but when I'd help him over to her bed, I'd see this wonderful smile come over her face. She could no longer see him, so she was responding to the sound of her husband coming near and crawling into bed beside her. She beamed when she felt his arms enfold her. They were a part of the blessed few—Master-Level Lovers.

I thought that scene was the sweetest, most beautiful thing I'd ever seen. After all these years, I still think that.

SEX AS SACRAMENT

As I mentioned in the first chapter, Dr. David Schnarch wrote one of my favorite scholarly books on sexuality and spirituality—*Constructing the Sexual Crucible*.[1] In it he talks about how rare it is for a couple to reach their sexual potential in marriage. If you are thinking this means accomplishing physical feats of gymnastic proportions in the bedroom—sex for the youthful and agile—you're missing Dr. Schnarch's meaning altogether. In fact, he jokingly proposes that the depth of sexual experience is directly proportional to the amount of a couple's cellulite and wrinkles. In other words, if a couple grows old together, accumulating layer after layer of experience with each other through life, and if they continue to learn to pull together in every storm, the sweetness of a kiss, the comfort of being held, and the dearness of making love only get deeper. It's got nothing to do with hard bodies. In fact, in my years of clinical observation, it is rare for people in their twenties to experience the kind of passion that a couple in their later years is capable of enjoying.

What I loved about Dr. Schnarch's research and theory is the mingling of sexuality and spirituality. I was a good Christian boy who hadn't experienced so much as a hug until I was well into my teens. When I read the words *sexuality* and *spirituality* in the same sentence, I had one of my biggest light-bulb moments as a Christian man and as a marriage therapist. Now I understand it to be one of the major keys to successful marriages.[2]

Once couples understand and regularly apply the major keys to proactive passion, their marriages cannot help but improve. Those three keys are:

1. Combining healthy spirituality with sexuality. (I don't like to separate the two because they go together—pardon my Forrest Gump expression—"like peas and carrots." People just cannot enjoy the best sex life possible without a healthy spiritual view of sex.)
2. Bringing your best and most balanced brains to the marriage. (I'll explain this in the next few chapters.)
3. Practicing four basic spiritual virtues and nurturing them into a near art form. (You'll read about these in the last chapter.)

In the next five chapters, we'll spend a lot of time exploring the five different brain types that enhance and complicate relationships, invaluable information I've learned from Dr. Daniel Amen, pioneer brain researcher and wonderful friend. But we'll begin here with a look at sexuality and spirituality because these are two ingredients that will enhance every single marriage, no matter your brain type. Without fail, these two elements have been there in every exceptional marriage I've observed. They are the foundation for becoming one of the "blissfully wedded" for a lifetime, part and parcel of becoming the blessed few. (If you happen to be depressed at the moment, you may not be excited about sex with your mate right now. But tuck this information away in the corners of your heart and mind, because once you begin to feel even some of your depression lift, you can begin to feel excited about applying the God-blessed balm of sexual healing to your marriage.)

It is so marvelous to realize how wise and creative God was when he thought up the concept of sex as a way to regularly bring couples back to one another—to help them reexperience the chemicals of joy and comfort that flood their brains and bodies with feel-good hormones. Regularly enjoying a healthy sexual relationship provides the glue that bonds a man and woman together, and frankly, it also acts like a balm to every other part of life. If a man and wife are happy in the bedroom, small irritations tend to turn into endearments rather than fodder for perpetual fights.

In part, this is because a brain-on-sex is enhanced by an internal love potion. Every time you enjoy touching or kissing or having passionate sex with the person you love, hormones are released that flood you with energy for life and passion for the day. Yes, this is why a man, soon after making love, may want to get up and tackle a difficult project or face some other giant task. Your love has filled him up, and he is ready to "kill the bear" now. Or if he is tired, he is totally relaxed and goes into peaceful sleep. And scientists have discovered that semen may have antidepressant qualities. After intercourse, women tend to feel relaxed and even euphoric with less physical and emotional pain. It's "good medicine" all around!

Sex for sex's sake, however, or sex with yourself or a stranger, does not produce the healthy high that sex-with-committed-love-in-marriage produces. It's "scratching an itch," but without the component of a sacred, committed relationship, sex never deeply satisfies your soul.

Growing up as a Christian, I understood at an intellectual level that God created man and woman, and it was good. I also knew that he created sex and it, too, was good. But it wasn't until a young Jewish woman and her Gentile husband came into my office for help with their marriage that I realized that our Christian culture has missed out on much of the power of combining the sacred and the sexual in our marriages as part of everyday life. Both of them were Christians, but she was raised in a strong Jewish tradition. At this point they had been married a number of years, and in short, nothing was now happening between them sexually.

"Tell me a little about your background," I said to the young woman. She explained that her father had moved to the States from Israel in the late 1940s and married her mom, who was Southern Baptist. She grew up in the Southwest. So on Saturdays she went alone to the temple, and on Sundays they went to church together.

When she was around twelve years old, she chose to give her life to Christ at her Baptist church. But she always kept the practice of going to the temple on Saturday as well and stayed highly involved with this culture because these were her father's roots. When she grew up, she actually went back to her father's homeland at one point, becoming a paratrooper for

Israel. I looked at this petite woman and tried to imagine her wielding a machine gun. Needless to say, her story held my interest.

And as I listened, the Holy Spirit seemed to guide my listening and helped me understand her heart at a deeper level. I looked at her and said, "It must be kind of hard for you to be around all us westernized Gentiles who are often prone to studying God through our intellect rather than experiencing God through our emotions. Your personality type seems to feel closest to God when your heart and feelings are fully engaged. Am I right?"

I don't know exactly what I said that opened the floodgates, but she started to sob. "Oh, Dr. Henslin, you have no idea how I miss my temple back home." She continued to weep, as if her heart had been in grief for years, and finally, she had permission and a safe place to let go. She longed for a type of connection to God and to others that she'd experienced in Jewish worship. Perhaps you'll remember the scene from *Fiddler on the Roof* where the men joyfully celebrate life, singing and dancing, "To life! To life! *L'chaim!*" or the unbridled emotion in *My Big Fat Greek Wedding*. The marriage ceremony had its time for solemnity, but was soon followed by singing, laughing, dancing, even weeping for happiness. These sorts of emotive celebrations were the way this young wife best experienced God's love. And it was also a clue to how she'd hoped to receive earthly love from her mate.

I glanced over at her poor husband. He was stunned, never having seen tears pour out of his wife like this. So I said to him, "Could you tell me a little bit more about what's going on sexually?" The husband began to describe their sex life in very cut-and-dried terms. Like an engineer. This happened and then that happened and then . . . it stopped happening altogether.

All of a sudden she sat up and said, "This is what's wrong with us! I grew up in the temple learning that being sexual with your husband is a wonderful spiritual and joyous time. You approach it from one angle—the physical." I nodded and encouraged her to keep sharing. "Okay, in a Jewish marriage, you might talk while you're making love; you might sing, you might pray! I mean, there are all kinds of things that happen. You laugh. You know, it's like this full-body experience! You don't leave your soul at the door—you bring it into the bedroom and party with it, inviting your body to follow!"

Again, I looked over at her husband and suddenly felt a rush of empathy for him. He could not have married a woman any more opposite from his own personality. I understood because he was originally from the Midwest. I'm from Minnesota, and we both come from a long line of stoics. To his passionate, dark-eyed wife, I said, "You know, you've got to be a little patient with us white Anglo-Saxon Protestants. Your view of sensuality is not quite the vision of sex we guys grew up with in our church."

Turning toward the husband, I said, "When she starts to talk or laugh or get playful, I bet you lose your erection." He lowered his head and said, "Doc, you got that right." Then I said, very gently to his wife, "Well, you'll just have to kind of bring him along a little easier. Help him understand your heart, but try to understand his as well."

The next week he came into my office, eyes wide, and said, "I don't know what's going on. She's not moping at all anymore. In fact, she's painting a mural on the wall and singing, and generally seems so much happier."

"So things must be better in the bedroom?" I queried.

He blushed and nodded. "They are, indeed. Once I understood where she was coming from, it was actually wonderful to experience lovemaking as more than a one-dimensional act."

These lovers moved a little bit closer to understanding each other as the husband was willing to see what sex meant to her, and she to realize that he didn't come with her viewpoint on sex automatically attached to his brain. They'd have to share, talk, learn, reach out, be patient, and grow—to apply all the fruits of the Spirit to their lovemaking. Sex became a very spiritual experience for both of them.

The Old Testament writers used the phrase "They knew each other" to describe when a couple had sexual relations. But in the Hebrew mind what this phrase meant was this: *When a couple makes love, each time they come to know each other a little bit more deeply.* Their bodies and their souls meet. They are playmates and soul mates. And as God said, it is very good.

Have you ever had a soulish experience during sex? Where you look into each others' eyes and maybe one of you even begins to cry? Our bodies are wired to connect our hearts. This is why all the sex substitutes leave us aching for something else. Cheap sex never satisfies. Soul sex, however—now, that is a gourmet experience.

WHAT WE CAN LEARN FROM JEWISH TRADITION

That session prompted me to do a bit more searching into our Jewish roots and culture for something we Gentiles perhaps left behind as we became Christians. I found that mutual love, desire, and sex in marriage are considered a *mitzvah*. What's a mitzvah? It is similar to our word for *sacrament*. Baptism is one of our holy sacraments, for example. Well, in the Jewish faith, a mitzvah is a kind of holy act or ritual, like prayer. In Judaism, sex between a husband and wife is a mitzvah; it is a holy act, and its purpose is to reinforce their loving bond. Here's a sampling of some of the teachings of rabbis regarding sex in marriage that I came upon and found fascinating:

- A man must never force his wife to have sex.
- A husband and wife may never have sex while drunk or quarreling.
- It's a serious offense to use sex to punish or manipulate a spouse.
- Sex is a woman's right, and not a man's right.
- Man has a duty to give sex to his wife regularly and ensure that sex is pleasurable for her.
- Sex may never be used as a weapon, either to deprive mates of it or compel them to have sex. No pushy persuasions, no threats. Using sex as a manipulation simply would be seen as wrong and sinful.
- The man is obligated to watch for signs of his wife's wanting touching, intimacy, and consummation—and to offer her pleasure without her having to ask.
- Sex is one of the woman's three basic rights in marriage, which a husband may not reduce.
- The Talmud specifies the quality and quantity of sex that a man must give his wife.
- A husband may not vow to abstain from sex for an extended period of time.
- A husband's consistent refusal to engage in sexual relations is grounds for divorce.
- On the other hand, while sex is a woman's right, she does not have absolute discretion to withhold it from her husband.
- A man may not take a journey for an extended period of time

because that would deprive the wife of a sexual relationship. In fact, I found one ancient text that said if a man had an opportunity to earn more money, but it would mean traveling away from his wife rather than working around the village, she had the right to tell him no. If she didn't want him to go because it would destroy or weaken the marital bond, he could not go.[3]

I was reading a book by a modern-day rabbi, and he was counseling a man who traveled for a living. The man asked him about the practicality of masturbating for sexual relief when he was often so far from home. The rabbi said, basically, "If you're having that kind of struggle, isn't that God's way of telling you that you're away from home too long?"

I loved the rabbi's answer: if that's a struggle for you, get home. Besides, as I jokingly ask my clients, "Does anyone really win at Solitaire?" Another alternative I would suggest is, if your wife is able to travel, take her with you. Most women love a chance to enjoy a hotel, room service, and new sights.

Of course, many of the ancient laws sound crazy to a modern ear. And I am not suggesting that Christians should follow all of these principles. But I am suggesting that a good look into Jewish practices and cultures could help us round out our Christian views of marriage, particularly pertaining to sexuality and spirituality. What I found particularly insightful and surprising was that in Judaism the women are raised to value their libidos and to see themselves as highly sensual creatures who will need and want to be pleasured regularly by their husbands. They see sex as a joyful, holy, and sacred act—honoring to God. The general view of the culture is that a woman's hunger is greater than that of a man's. I don't know about you, but this is not what I was taught in my Christian-based premarital Sunday-school class.

However, I have grown to believe that the Jewish culture is right on this issue. When a couple begins to operate along these guidelines: "sex is joyful and sacred"; "a man needs to be attentive to a woman's desire and strive to meet her needs"; "it is never used for manipulation but only 'knowing each other' more deeply, body and soul," well, women begin to line up for that kind of sex with their husbands! They become hungry for lovers who satisfy them at a soul level.

Writing this chapter made me think about the Jewish couples I've worked with over the years. Many of them have come in and they might be fussing, arguing, and even yelling at each other, as many couples do when they finally get desperate enough to seek help for a problem. But when I ask them about their sexual relationship, they often look at me as if to say, "Well, why would there be anything wrong with our sex life?" That's because sex is considered to be such a holy act that to not be sexual in marriage is like saying, "I am not going to pray." It's rather unthinkable.

I remember once going out to the waiting room to meet a teenage client. She was in opposition, defiant, and explosive at home. Her mother had recently remarried after her husband, the girl's beloved father, had died of cancer. I saw that the teenager was reading a prayer book in Hebrew. I just watched her for a few seconds, this girl whom the mom said was struggling in school but was now totally engrossed with her prayer book. An idea sprang to mind.

When the mother and daughter came in to the session, I said to the daughter, "Would you read one of those prayers aloud to me?"

She looked puzzled, then said, "You're a Christian, aren't you?"

"Yeah," I replied. "I think we're worshiping the same God as far as I know." And so she looked down, took a breath, and read a prayer to me. I wept. It was so moving, watching this teenager who was so hard and angry transformed before my eyes as she read that old, old prayer. She read with a kind of melodic, rhythmic tone to her voice, and I could tell it was coming from deep within her. When she read this prayer, she experienced it from deep in her soul, and even I felt it.

I learned that her father would come into his daughter's room and read poetry or scripture every night before they went to bed. Now this girl deeply missed her father. He left behind shoes that would be difficult for any man to fill. A new man on the scene could not live up to her wonderful memory of the daddy she loved and lost.

There are moments in a therapist's office when I feel as if I know nothing, that I am just there as a silent witness to the miracle of two people connecting deeply. This was one of those moments. The mother looked lovingly at her daughter and said very softly, as if she were speaking an ancient truth directly into the heart of her child, "I know you miss your father. And someday you'll understand this better. But God designed us to couple. We are here to couple and partner on this earth."

We are here to "couple." In that sentence, this mother gave me the word I'd been searching for: a word to describe the mingling of the soul—of the spiritual and the sexual in marriage. I am teaching husbands and wives to "couple" as a calling from God, as a sacred act.

There is a Jewish custom called *Shabbat* that I especially love. On Friday nights as the sun goes down, it signals the beginning of *Shabbat*, the time of preparation for worship on Sabbath morning, which would be Saturday morning. Eighteen minutes before sundown, the woman of the house begins lighting candles. The candles represent a time of romance with God. Isn't that beautiful? Children are taught that intimacy with God—the feeling part of growing in love with God and experiencing his love—is worth celebrating with candlelight, dressing up, and having a special meal.

Then when the husband comes home, he sees those candles, and he is smiling—he knows that this time of intimacy and prayer with God will naturally lead to gratitude and intimacy with his wife later.

The family then gathers around the dinner table. The husband reads scriptures and prays. The wife and children do the same. The whole family is involved in this. Some of the prayers are thanking God for the wine and the bread, which is a lovely precursor, I think, to the Christian communion. Then the husband goes and stands behind his wife, places his hands on her shoulders, and sings Proverbs 31 over her. "Who can find a virtuous wife? For her worth is far above rubies" (v. 10). And if he can't sing, he reads this passage over her.

The purpose? To remind himself and his children about the good things his wife brings to their lives. Then he prays a blessing over her, thanking God for her love and care. Okay, I am going to go out on a limb here and guess that if most women were thus honored every Friday night, they would be itching to get such a loving leader of a man alone in their beds later. And in fact, this is exactly what happens.

Later in the privacy of their room, the couple reads portions of the Song of Songs to each other and makes love. In fact, the ancient rabbis would give a benediction encouraging all the married couples to make love on *Shabbat* as preparation for worship Sabbath morning. Wouldn't you love to hear that from your pastor?

Recently I shared some of the above information with a client, and she just started laughing. Just about fell off the couch. I grinned. "What are you laughing about?"

"I just now figured something out!" she exclaimed. "When I was in elementary school, my favorite girlfriend was Jewish. I just loved it when I stayed over at her house on Friday nights. Every Friday night we would have dinner in the dining room, and the best china was out. Her dad would come home from work, and then he'd go upstairs and shower and completely change into a nice outfit. Then her mom would go upstairs, shower, and come down in a beautiful dress, and I remember she wore a lacy veil over her face.

"The moment her mom stepped into the dining room, her dad got up, pulled out a chair, and she sat down. I just loved watching him being so gallant to his wife. And then came prayers and scriptures. When we finished dinner, we watched her parents go upstairs, arm in arm, gazing at each other like lovesick teenagers. The kids would then start giggling as they took the plates into the kitchen and started washing dishes, as they'd been taught to do on Fridays. Now I know what they were giggling about!"

Can you imagine the lessons those kids were taught in that wonderful household? They saw how a man should value and treat a woman. They observed the honor a woman receives from her husband, and thus, the message he imparted to the children was that she is worthy of their respect and kindness. They enjoyed watching the marvelous mingling of food, laughter, gratitude to God, and romance between married people who know the art of coupling. What my client learned on those Friday nights by sheer observation I have spent years trying to help couples comprehend in the counseling office.

I have dozens of fascinating scientific studies I could quote you about how a healthy sex life leads to happy, healthy people who live long lives. I could have spent most of this chapter describing sexual techniques and exercises. But my desire was, instead, to paint you a picture, borrowed from a culture that knows how to mix the spiritual and the sexual into a healthy blend of marital happiness.

For those who have been sexually abused and never understood how God created sex for good, I hope you've caught a glimpse of his original intention for sex in marriage. If you've been raised to be a good Christian girl and wonder how to integrate sexuality with holiness, I pray this chapter starts you thinking of lovemaking from God's view. Becoming a sensual and sexual wife is one of the most beautiful "arts of home" that most mothers neglect to teach their daughters.

If you are a man and are frustrated because you "aren't getting any at home," I hope you've caught a glimpse of the kind of husband you can become, who helps nurture and honor a wife so beautifully, and that you will be too busy pleasing her to look around at anyone else. You may not orchestrate a formal *Shabbat* in your home, but if you can borrow even a few elements or adopt some of the attitudes shared here, perhaps you'll begin to experience a joining of bodies and souls as you make love with all the gratitude your hearts can hold.

There is science behind everything I've said in this chapter and much more to come in the pages before us. But even science is at a loss for words to describe what happens when spirituality and sexuality invade the hearts of true lovers such as Henry and Martha. And hopefully, masterful lovers like you and your sweetheart.

Aspire to be a part of the blessed few, and you'll never regret it.

> *Many waters cannot quench love,*
> *nor can rivers drown it.*
> *If a man tried to buy love*
> *with all his wealth,*
> *his offer would be utterly scorned.*
> —Song of Solomon 8:7 NLT

CHAPTER THREE

Bring Your Best Brain to the Marriage!

Marriage can be hard. It tends to be much more successful
when the brains of both partners function in a healthy way.

—DR. DANIEL AMEN

Soul is a beautiful word. Though I must say, it's a word that has been overused in the American book publishing industry over the last decade or so. It began with *Chicken Soup for the Soul*, which spawned hundreds of variations on the mega-bestselling series with titles such as *Pasta for the Italian Lover's Soul, Yarns for the Knitter's Soul, Chocolate-Covered Prozac for the PMSing Soul, Antacids for the Flatulent Soul*, and so on. Okay, I'm making up these titles, but you get the gist.

But in the original Hebrew language, the word *soul* was unique and rich in meaning, summing up our thoughts, feelings, personality characteristics, needs, and desires. It was a wonderful, all-encompassing word that described who we essentially are from the tops of our heads to the bottoms of our feet.[1]

Another spin-off phrase that has buzzed its way around therapists' offices, self-help seminars, and clergy from all denominations is the term *soul care*. To care for my own soul means to take responsibility for all of who I am. It's to nurture, protect, mature, and heal my own "thoughts, feelings, personality characteristics, needs, and desires." Obviously, we do this in partnership with the Holy Spirit, and it is a lifelong process of blossoming into your truest, most authentic and God-ordained self.

If we don't take 100 percent responsibility for the care and feeding of our own souls, we will never bring our healthiest selves to any relationship, but it is especially critical in our most intimate relationship: marriage. Ultimately, to abandon the care of your own soul is to neglect your spouse. Let me say that again: *to abandon the care of your own soul is to flatly neglect your spouse and your marriage.* And one aspect of the soul that I am most concerned about, that I believe couples are unwittingly neglecting, is the care of their brains. So, I'll often tell couples coming in for marriage counseling, "Along with learning to mingle spirituality with sexuality and get your love life on track, the other step in your becoming a proactively passionate couple is to have your heads examined." Then I wait for their eyes to widen and their mouths to drop open and at least one of them to look for the nearest exit. But I *do* have their attention.

SOUL CARE INCLUDES BRAIN CARE

Thousands of books have been written about how to have happier marriages. There are some great volumes on the subject of dealing with the emotional baggage we all haul into matrimony with us—positive psychology and solution-focused books with a plethora of practical ideas to improve our relationships. There are tons that help with sexual techniques, nutrition, and physical fitness. However, precious few books come at the marriage relationship and its troublesome patches by taking time to address the brain health of both parties. You are holding just such a book in your hands right now.

Here's why I believe this is the first book that couples should read when they face an impasse. Most of the above forms of help for married couples are amazingly effective and work beautifully with two people whose brains are pretty balanced. Good, intuitive, experienced therapists want as many tools in their toolbox as they can gather, to help people in a variety of situations. But in my experience, brain improvement isn't just a therapist's tool; it's the *toolbox.* Without this foundational information—looking at the emotional health of each brain in the relationship—the great tools a therapist is attempting to use may be falling and failing and dropping to the floor. And though I believe the earlier chapters you've just read about sexuality and spirituality are all important, I also know that many brains that aren't functioning well cannot engage in beautiful soul sex.

Yet.

In my practice, after a thorough intake, I will address possible brain imbalances before encouraging my clients to dive into the bed with each other. But as soon as they are feeling better, I suggest they resume their sexual activity—because beautiful lovemaking helps everything else they'll learn and apply in therapy to go much better.

I've found that when my brain or your brain isn't working right, in all honesty, we may as well toss out the rest of the physical improvement, self-help, or spiritual-growth books on our shelves. That may sound like an overstatement, but then, you've never walked in my particular marriage-therapist shoes and seen what I've seen. Trying to help some patients change without first fixing their brain imbalances is like trying to get software to work on a computer whose hard drive is faulty.

In fact, let me invite you into my therapist's office to be a fly on the couch, so to speak. Before me, we have Ed, who doesn't know that his episodes of uncontrollable rage and his underlying irritation and hair-trigger suspicion actually stem from a long-ago injury in his temporal lobes. (Don't worry about what these brain terms mean right now; we'll get to them. Just go with me here.) He's here with his wife, Gloria, who has the look of one of those poor, weary lab rats who has been shocked randomly one too many times. Her eyes have a glazed, tired, faraway look, and when I ask how she feels, she says, "I don't know." In the past I might have prodded her to uncover her pent-up feelings, but you know what? I actually believe her. I don't think she has a clue how she is feeling, except for maybe a vague numbness to most deep feelings—good or bad. From the answers to her intake questions I see that she's likely depressed and I imagine her limbic system is overactive, which means that she's probably not had a sexual thought in a long time. (We have a saying around here: "When your limbic is hot—showing too much brain activity—you are not.")

I ask Ed how he is feeling and why he is here. Though I can see it takes effort for him to describe their issues in a civil way, it isn't long before he basically barks out some version of, "I'm mad as hell, and I am not going to take it anymore!"

"Why do you think you are so angry?" I ask, forcing myself not to back my chair away a couple of inches.

"She's always egging me on! All I ask for is a decent supper at five o'clock, and half the time I come home, she's napping on the couch. I mean, what's she doing all day that she's got to sleep when I come home? The other half of the time, she's pulling a limp frozen dinner out of the microwave. So I end up yelling at her, which does absolutely no good. I grab a beer to calm my nerves, flip on the TV for the next few hours, and head to bed, hoping for a little, you know, *action*. But she's usually beat me to bed, her back is turned to me, and she's sawing logs. How much of this rejection can a guy take before he lashes out? Yeah, I'm angry! What does she expect?"

I glance toward Gloria, who looks as though she'd love nothing more than a long nap somewhere on the other side of the world from Ed.

In the old days of doing therapy, I might have talked about where Ed's anger may have originated as a child and eventually given Ed "homework assignments" to basically help him work on being kinder and more patient. At some point, I'd ask Gloria if she could compromise, maybe try a little harder to get up off the couch and encourage her husband. I'd give them assignments for the week that I would hope against hope might help them reconnect. We'd pray for the Lord to help them forgive, to change, to reach out to one another.

However, after nearly thirty years of practice, I know that most couples such as Ed and Gloria—particularly those who have been married for decades—have poor relational habits that are practically set in stone by the time they come to therapy. Habitual responses are ingrained deep in their brains by this time. I know it is doubtful that Ed and Gloria will feel much better or even be slightly more in love with months of weekly sessions. Oh, I may have a breakthrough here and there, and they may seem lovey-dovey as they leave my office, but more often than not, by the time they are in the car on the way home, old painful patterns will start up again. Of course, I could make a lot of money off of this unhappily wedded couple as long as they are willing to come and see me. But then, eventually, they'd depress *me*, and I'd have to let them go for my own sanity.

Today, after a routine intake in the above scenario, I would ask Ed and Gloria to save some of their money on talk therapy with me and give some of it, instead, to someone else. I'd ask them each to consider getting a SPECT brain scan (more on this soon) from a qualified neurologist, and after that was done, I'd schedule an appointment to go through their results together. Then I would honestly tell them, "If I can get a peek at your brains, and you will both work with me and a physician to balance out any organic mood issues that show up, we can shorten the time you'd spend with me in marriage therapy by at least half and double your chances of living happily ever after, together. Or at least enjoy happily ever after more often than not."

To become a member of the blessed few—or what expert marriage researcher John Gottman calls the "masters of marriage"[2]—couples need to have full access to the parts of their brains that temper anger with humor and compassion, that allow for concentration along with give-and-take listening, that keep disagreements from careening out of control, and that help calm addictive urges.

Marriage therapists know what a good relationship looks like and are wonderful at giving couples goals to work toward. Why, then, hasn't the divorce rate changed? Why is the success rate of marriage therapy so dismal? It's generally accepted that most marriage therapy helps only about 25 to 50 percent of the time (depending on whose study you read), and in many cases couples feel that therapy made things worse. What kind of odds are these? In my opinion, therapists are not very good at helping the individual spouses to balance their personal temperaments so they can become the sort of mates who can function and enjoy being part of an intimate pair. Ignoring the everyday reality of malfunctioning brains is the pink elephant in the room of modern marriage therapy.

IT'S NOT FOR LACK OF EFFORT

In my marriage practice, I'd say that the two most common reasons for divorce are anger problems and sexual issues. Often there is some kind of sexual addiction or affair, as well as lingering issues of childhood sexual abuse.

Anger and sexual malfunctions happen to some of the most physically fit, health food–eating, sincerely religious, positive-thinking, intelligent, motivated, and hard-praying people I know. Their recurring battles or "besetting sins" are not happening for a lack of desire to change or shortage of earnest effort. Unless you live on a remote island, you've probably seen the now-famous *Saturday Night Live* skit with then Republican vice presidential nominee Sarah Palin, expertly played by Tina Fey, and Hillary Clinton, played by comedian Amy Poehler. You may remember "Hillary's" breakdown as she responds to an insinuation by "Sarah" that perhaps Hillary just didn't want the presidency (or vice presidency) enough. At this point, Hillary's *SNL* caricature loses it. Her teeth clenched, eyes wild, she begins clawing off portions of the podium at the frustrating absurdity of the accusation.

When well-meaning pastors preach sermon after sermon to their parishioners about how they can change if they simply want it enough, or pray hard enough, or try more this week . . . I imagine the caricature of Hillary in that *SNL* skit having a public meltdown. Believe me, most people are not failing to get victory over their unwanted behaviors because they aren't trying hard enough to change. In fact, most men and women who battle anger, fear, addictions, and a myriad of other challenging emotions are actually some of the world's most tenderhearted and sensitive people at the core of their souls.

Then what's the problem? In my experience, therapy- and prayer-resistant problems stem from an imbalance in the brain. Whether the imbalance got there because of genetics or experience, nature or nurture, I sometimes can't say for sure. However, with the brain scan, I often discover that there has been a physical injury to the brain. Even something as mild as an old playground or football injury to the head can cause lifelong problems with anger, focus, and a myriad of other issues. But that's more information for future chapters.

YOUR BEST BRAIN NOW

What I want to do in this chapter is to plant the seed in your mind that to be proactively passionate, to have an exceptional marriage, *you have to take responsibility for bringing your best, healthiest, most balanced brain to your marriage.* When two people work toward having their brains more balanced and when their emotions begin to normalize, often the need for marriage therapy simply evaporates. And if it doesn't evaporate, then the couple is much more able to absorb information and implement changes that I suggest. Once this balancing has taken place, marriage education, coaching, or therapy becomes very effective. It's like the difference between teaching a child with two healthy legs how to walk and teaching someone with a broken leg to walk.

Dr. Daniel G. Amen, the pioneer of SPECT brain-scan research, best-selling author, and host of a series of PBS specials on brain health, says in nearly all of his lectures, "When your brain works right, *you* work right." The story of how I met Dr. Amen and began to integrate brain scans into my therapy practice has been told in depth in my first book, *This Is Your Brain on Joy.* But the nutshell version is that fifteen years ago I heard Dr. Amen speak on how brain health affects our moods, behaviors, and thus, our happiness and relationships in profound ways. Unable to shake off what I learned in that seminar, I dived in and, like a hungry sponge, learned everything I could about the brain from Dr. Amen over the next fifteen years, sending hundreds of patients to the Amen Clinic for help. As a result, the success rate of helping my clients began to soar. They got better faster, and their results were more permanent and lasting. (For more details on SPECT scans, see the appendices.)

A HEAD CHECK

How do we begin to take responsibility for our brain health? First, we have to take a look under the hood of your head, so to speak, and learn about the five mood centers that affect your emotions and therefore your marriage—from moment to moment. Did you know that psychiatry is the only medical field where we do not routinely look at what's happening inside the body that may be causing a persistent problem? Would you trust a doctor who said, "I think you've broken some bone in your arm, so I'm going to just take a wild stab at this and guess which bone is *probably* broken. Then I'll set it, put a cast on it, send you home, and we'll just hope for the best. Okey-dokey?" No, you'd insist on an X-ray, and probably forthwith, find another doctor. Or how about a physician who suspected you might have a brain tumor or an appendix that might rupture and he decides to write you out a prescription for "positive thinking exercises"—based on your best hopes—to help ease your pain. Ridiculous. You'd insist on an MRI and any other tests they might have so that you could see what's happening inside your body and best know exactly how to remedy it in the fastest way possible.

Once I learned about brain imaging and saw the inner workings of my clients' brains, along with the wealth of information this gave me to help them, the field of "modern" psychotherapy—and in particular, marriage therapy—seemed tragically arcane to me. We are playing guessing games with people's emotional lives and, as a result, are not helping marriages succeed as we could and should.

Does this mean that every person needs a brain scan in order to be happily married? Though it might be *interesting* and even helpful if this could happen, of course, not everyone needs a brain scan, any more than people with healthy bodies need an X-ray. However, with every client who comes into my office, I always use the Amen Brain Subsystems Checklist to help me determine what is probably happening inside the client's brain. You'll be able to take applicable portions of this test at the beginning of each of the next several chapters. Over the years, I have been amazed at how closely this intake reflects what we would find in an actual brain scan. From the intake, I can offer a variety of ways to help calm or perk up brain imbalances with dietary tweaks, supplements, exercise, changes in environment, and other therapeutic activities. But if we find this isn't doing the trick, and I suspect something more complicated is going on, where medication might even be helpful, I will suggest a brain scan. I don't want to play around with suggestions for medication, and with a SPECT scan, we can see what the patient needs with pinpoint accuracy. My office works with the Amen Clinics to try to make this as affordable as possible for my clients. However, the written tests in this book usually correspond with amazing accuracy to the brain scans we see. Not everyone needs to go to the expense of a brain scan; but it is a very powerful tool in complicated or resistant cases.

In my experience there are five brain imbalances that affect a person's ability to be the best partner he or she can possibly be in a marriage. Many times a person will have more than one area that needs calmed or corrected since some of them overlap. For simplicity's sake, I've summarized them into five imbalanced lover types. (Keep in mind that most of us have moments of imbalance, so even if your issues are mild, you'll find help to improve your daily experience of joy and peace—making you an even better partner.)

1. The Scattered Lover
2. The Overfocused Lover
3. The Blue Mood Lover
4. The Agitated Lover
5. The Anxious Lover

We'll be discussing each of these lover types in detail in the chapters to come, but in brief, the summaries below will help you recognize yourself or your mate. Also, please realize that one or both of you may be a combination of types, as is often the case.

THE SCATTERED LOVER

The Scattered Lover tends to come in two different forms. One is the hyperactive, bouncy, all-over-the-place version. They are high in energy and low on attention—unless they are very, very fascinated by something in their environment. Then they can become extremely focused. Many spouses of mates with attention deficit disorder are frustrated by their husbands' or wives' ability to focus on a video game or hobby they love, but can't maintain or engage in a focused give-and-take conversation or hear and act upon simple requests. They seem to have endless energy, until they crash.

The second type of Scattered Lover is the classic absentminded professor. They're often smart, but just as often lost in their own world. For example, Einstein, who discovered the theory of relativity, but never seemed to find a decent comb. Or if he did, forgot to use it on his wild, white mane. These people are typically pleasant, but so easily caught up in watching the flowers bloom, they are often late for things like doctor's appointments and planes taking off. Sweet-tempered but maddening for mates who prefer punctuality to last-minute panic, and order to creative chaos. (Or "comfy cluttered nests," as they often prefer to call their messy offices and bedrooms.)

THE OVERFOCUSED LOVER

These are the classic people who are like a dog with a bone once they get stuck on a thought. They have a very hard time shifting their set-in-stone perspectives because their viewpoint feels unalterably right and comforting. They can range from a mate who cannot forgive an offense from years ago, to one who gets fixated on an activity (good or bad) and can't stop, to one who has compulsive tendencies (to check locks or count cracks in the sidewalk or overparent). The far end of this spectrum would include people with obsessive-compulsive disorder, with the mid-range being seen as control freaks, with the less severe end of this continuum including people who just have a very hard time letting go of being right or shifting from one project to another or one idea to another.

THE BLUE MOOD LOVER

Blue moods happen to all of us at some time or another, particularly after any kind of loss. PMS or adrenal burnout can plummet the sunniest of dispositions into a blue mood. However, many people seem to have been born with a gloomy outlook. You try to point out that the glass is half-full, and they'll not only declare it half-empty but also point out that the glass is smeared and has a small chip in it, and the water tastes a little funky, as well. They look for the worst in everything and seem to take a certain pride in discovering What Could Go Wrong first and sharing it with anyone who might listen. If you've ever had an unrelenting pessimist-type on your team, you may have experienced a slow, sure drain in your own energy.

Negativity can become habitual and to some people is as addicting as alcohol. Someone with a true, deep, chemical depression is different from one who has learned negative behavior by osmosis, usually from growing up in a negative family environment. You know the commercials on TV that say, "Depression hurts everywhere"? (These commercials are *so* depressing!) Well, depression also hurts everyone who loves you. If you are suffering from a chronic low mood, your first priority, before working on your marriage, would be to become *radically proactive* about uncovering the source of your sadness and getting the right help for it. We'll spend an entire chapter talking about the variety of issues that can cause you to feel sad and how to get you or your mate back on the sunny side of the street.

THE AGITATED LOVER

The spouse of an easily agitated or angered mate will nearly always say, "I have to walk on eggshells in my own home." When a person is easily irritated or angered—unusually so—I've found there is nearly always a biochemical component to this issue. In fact, as I pointed out in my earlier book, *This Is Your Brain on Joy*, I treated thirty couples where one of them had an anger issue so severe that I suspected an underlying brain issue. I sent all to have a SPECT scan, and they were given various treatments according to their specific biological needs. Ten years later, twenty-nine out of the thirty couples are still happily married. One man refused to follow the treatment plan and his marriage, sadly, ended in divorce. So the bad news is that an anger problem is one of the most destructive of marital issues. The good news? It's now one of the most easily corrected problems.

THE ANXIOUS LOVER

Many of us come to the table of marriage with a long string of old wounds. Without meaning to, we may accidentally trigger an old trauma in our spouse, who has suffered from some kind of abuse, neglect, or sudden tragic loss. People who have had trauma in their past often become hypervigilant—on the lookout for anything that might hurt them again. It's a bit like living with Chicken Little—trying to reassure them over and over that the sky is not falling; it's just a cloud passing by. People become anxious lovers in one of two ways: they were hurt or traumatized in the past, or they were simply born with a brain that is prone to anxiety. Anxiety, fear, and panic often run in families. We'll explore ways to calm the hypervigilant anxiety center in a future chapter.

Now that you've been briefly introduced to the five imbalanced lover types, let's explore each one in more depth and find some solutions for each one, which will help you bring your best brain to the union of your marriage. You are well on your way to creating a marriage of proactive passion.

Before each chapter there will be a little test to see if you may have some tendencies toward being the particular lover type under discussion.

On page 36 is a cartoon drawing of the brain that will help you locate the general areas of the brain that contribute to the five basic mood imbalances. It's a very oversimplified chart of the five basic mood areas discussed in this book because I don't want to overwhelm you with brain science. So think of the chart as Brain 101. My goal is to make sure I can explain any neuroscience I use in my books to any client or listening audience and have them understand the terms easily. (*This Is Your Brain on Joy* goes into a bit more detail, if you find this subject interesting.)

The chart below and the graphic of the brain are my attempts to take Thoreau's advice and "simplify, simplify, simplify."

THE FIVE MOOD AREAS OF A BRAIN THAT NEEDS BALANCE

1. *The Scattered Lover*

   Brain area affected: Prefrontal Cortex (or PFC)

   Nicknamed: Presidential Control Center

   Description: Acts as the organization, decision, and conscience-guiding center.

2. *The Overfocused Lover*

   Brain area affected: Cingulate Gyrus

   Nicknamed: Circular Gerbil Wheel

   Description: When overactive, thoughts (usually negative ones) get stuck, like a gerbil looping around on a wheel.

3. *The Blue Mood Lover*

   Brain area affected: Deep Limbic System

   Nicknamed: Depressed/Low-Mood Area

Description: When overactive, blue moods, sadness, or depression reign in the brain.

4. *The Agitated Lover*

   Brain area affected: Temporal Lobes

   Nicknamed: Temper Lofts

   Description: When imbalanced, can cause a variety of mood problems, from very dark thoughts to unreasonable rages.

5. *The Anxious Lover*

   Brain area affected: Basil Ganglia

   Nicknamed: Basement of Giant Fears

   Description: When overactive, anxiety floods the brain. Usually one of the areas affected in post-traumatic stress disorder (PTSD).

The Brain House

When the Five Mood Centers (Rooms) Need Repair

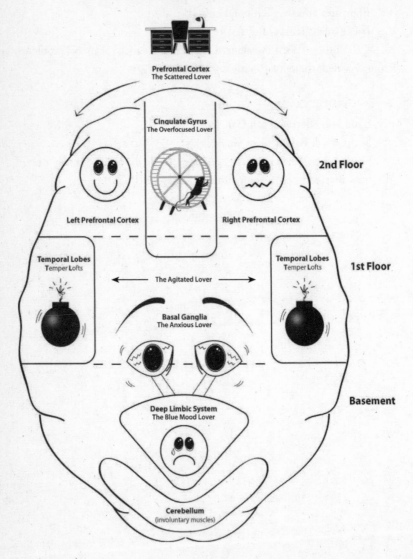

Prefrontal Cortex
The Scattered Lover

Cingulate Gyrus
The Overfocused Lover

2nd Floor

Left Prefrontal Cortex

Right Prefrontal Cortex

Temporal Lobes
Temper Lofts

1st Floor

The Agitated Lover

Temporal Lobes
Temper Lofts

Basal Ganglia
The Anxious Lover

Basement

Deep Limbic System
The Blue Mood Lover

Cerebellum
(involuntary muscles)

Please rate yourself on each of the symptoms listed below, using the following scale:

0=Never 1=Rarely 2=Occasionally 3=Frequently 4=Very Frequently
N/A=Not Applicable/Not Known
    (You answer in one column, your mate in the other column.)

____ ____ 1. Fail to give close attention to details or make careless mistakes

____ ____ 2. Have trouble sustaining attention in routine situations (i.e., housework, chores, paperwork)

____ ____ 3. Have trouble listening

____ ____ 4. Fail to finish things

____ ____ 5. Have poor organization for time or space (such as briefcase, room, desk, paperwork)

____ ____ 6. Avoid, dislike, or are reluctant to engage in tasks that require sustained mental effort

____ ____ 7. Lose things

____ ____ 8. Are easily distracted

____ ____ 9. Are forgetful

____ ____ 10. Have poor planning skills

____ ____ 11. Lack clear goals or forward thinking

____ ____ 12. Have difficulty expressing feelings

____ ____ 13. Have difficulty expressing empathy for others

____ ____ 14. Daydream excessively

____ ____ 15. Feel bored

____ ____ 16. Feel apathetic or unmotivated

____ ____ 17. Feel tired, sluggish, or slow moving

____ ____ 18. Feel spacey or in a fog

____ ____ 19. Are fidgety, restless, or have trouble sitting still

____ ____ 20. Have difficulty remaining seated in situations where remaining seated is expected

____ ____ 21. Are constantly on the go or act as if driven by a motor

_____ _____ 22. Talk excessively

_____ _____ 23. Blurt out answers before questions have been completed

_____ _____ 24. Have difficulty waiting your turn

_____ _____ 25. Interrupt or intrude on others (e.g., butt into conversations)

_____ _____ 26. Are impulsive (saying or doing things without thinking first)

Results: If nine or more symptoms are rated 3 or 4, this indicates a problem with the prefrontal cortex. (1 through 18 indicates a more "inattentive type" ADD; 19 through 26 may indicate ADHD, which includes symptoms of hyperactivity along with attention problems.)

From Amen Brain Subsystem Checklist, used by permission from Dr. Daniel Amen and the Amen Clinic.

CHAPTER FOUR

The Scattered Lover
(Prefrontal Cortex)

I prefer to distinguish ADD as attention abundance disorder. Everything is just so interesting . . . remarkably at the same time.

—FRANK COPPOLA, MA, ODC, ACG

If you've often been told to slow down, be still, focus, or be practical . . . you might be a Scattered Lover.

If you've bought a dozen organizers and proceeded to almost immediately lose them or leave them in a dozen different places . . . you might be a Scattered Lover.

If your mate has ever pulled his hair when you announced that, once again, you forgot to pick up the dry cleaning, or the milk, or the toddler from the babysitter . . . you might be a Scattered Lover.

If your beloved has ever banged her head against the wall or yelled, "You never listen! You never pay attention! Your eyes keep wandering around the room! You don't even see or hear me!" . . . well, you might be a Scattered Lover.

Welcome to my world. Or probably more accurately, welcome to my wife's world. I have always struggled with ADD (attention deficit disorder), which makes me pretty lovable and laid-back most of the time (I don't have hyperactivity with my attention deficit). But I'm highly . . . um . . . challenging for my wife and others at certain times. My mind often feels like a room full of bouncing ideas and thoughts, happening all at once—especially if I miss my meds.

Typical example of a day in the life of Dr. Earl: I thought that buying a laptop would be an improvement over the dismal failure of my forever-misplaced Day Planner. Surely, I couldn't forget a laptop! But this summer, I actually got a call from a kindhearted waitress at my favorite local café, letting me know that, yep, I'd left my laptop behind with the tip on the table.

Karen has had her share of hair-pulling with me as her mate. Why is it that messies continually marry neatniks? Morning people marrying night owls? We're drawn to our polar opposites and then settle down to live the rest of our lives with someone who, as my Texas friend says, "aggravates the far out of me!"

It helps both parties in a marriage to know that most of the time Scattered Lovers are just being unfocused (or overfocused, depending on your perspective) because they were made or wound up that way. They aren't bouncing around the room or forgetting things or dismissing your deep need to have things in their place and in working order—on purpose. They are truly unaware or distracted. And yes, often their focus is on silly things, but also quite often the Scattered Lovers of this world are compassionate, artistic, and off-the-wall creative. One of my favorite cases in point: the wildly successful and creative Hollywood director Steven Spielberg. A handful of quotes from his mother, Leah, about what life was like raising Steven give insight into the agony and ecstasy of living with and loving a scattered type. When asked if she always knew Steven was a genius, she admits she had no idea. "Frankly, I didn't know what the hell he was."[1] Why didn't she catch on that her son harbored brilliance? First of all, Steven was never a good student. When his teacher told Leah that he was "special," she just wondered what sort of euphemism that stood for.

Leah and her husband had a horrible time getting babysitters for their kids, unless they agreed not to leave Steven with them. Steven was the king of messy kids. Leah opined that "you could grow mushrooms on the floor" of his bedroom. His pet lizard once escaped "and we found it—three years later." He had a parakeet that he refused to put in a cage at all. "Once a week," said his mother, "I would stick my head in, grab his dirty laundry, and slam the door." Leah teases that maybe if she had known better in those days she might have taken him to a therapist, but "there would never have been an *E.T.*"

As fascinating as Steven was as a child, it is easy to see that this apple didn't fall far from his maternal grandparents' tree. And yes, Scattered Creatives often run in families. There's a strong genetic component. Leah herself never had a conventional childhood, which helped prepare her to be fairly nonchalant when Steven exploded cans of cherry pie filling in her kitchen to make a home horror movie. Leah's mother had a beautiful public speaking voice and was an amazing orator though domesticity was mostly hit-and-miss. "She was a marvelous lady who never mastered the can opener in her whole life."

Steven's grandfather was a Russian immigrant who struggled to make a living, but that isn't what Leah remembered most. She recalled her father in full-color memories and thought him very exciting. She remembered walking through a snowstorm with him once, and her father looked up at the glistening sky and quoted the psalmist: "How wondrous are thy works."

Through tear-filled eyes, Leah said, "How wondrous are thy works. This is who I am. This is who Steven is."[2]

To sum up, Scattered Lovers may have a hard time finding the floor, but their spouses know they are marvelous at pointing out the wonders in the sky.

Generally speaking, Scattered Lovers are the cheerleaders and encouragers of the world. And though they may forget to turn out the light or turn off the water or take their shoes to the closet, the best of them will never forget to kiss you good night or tell you they love you. Unless, that is, they have lost their bounce . . . and that is something nobody ever really wants to see happen. You do not want to be the mate who destroys the bounce in your ADD lover's step. You just want him or her to learn calming and focusing skills; and with help, your mate can do it.

INSIDE THE WINDOW OF AN ADD BRAIN

ADD and other focus problems generally begin in the prefrontal cortex. This is the area right behind your forehead, and it is the seat of logic and foresight, planning and contemplation. In other words, it controls all those attributes that fly out of your mind just when you probably need them most—in times of stress, high emotion, or need for focus—which is why impulsivity is one of the most common problems among our breed of human.

In fact, the way doctors discover that someone has ADD at the Amen Clinic is by giving him a little computer test that requires extended, concentrated focus. We consistently find that in folks without ADD symptoms, the blood in their brains naturally flows to where it is needed most: in their brain's control center or the prefrontal cortex. But in those with ADD—either the scatterbrained-but-laid-back kind or the hyperactive-jumping-and-fidgety kind—the blood simply leaves the front of the brain, especially when focus is required. It is a totally involuntary symptom over which they have no control. Some brains, when called upon to focus, tend to lose blood flow (or perfusion), and some tend to attract it. If you or your spouse has ADD, this may be an *aha* moment for you. *So that's why they zone out when I need to talk to them most of the time or leave a half dozen tasks half-finished or . . .* (fill in the blank with your own head-scratching frustration).

In order to understand more about the specific functions of the prefrontal cortex (PFC) let's look at the following chart:

Prefrontal Function	Prefrontal Cortex Problems
Focus	Jumps from topic to topic, will have difficulty staying with one topic until resolved.
Forethought	Before speaking and acting, inwardly unable to say, *Will this move me closer in relationship, away, or against?* There's a lack in the quality of mindfulness in what a person says and does.
Impulse Control	Seems unable to stop self from saying or doing things that sabotage relationships.
Organization	Difficulty putting order to his world. Often struggles to pay bills on time, live on budget, have a home or office that has order rather than chaos.
Planning	Struggles to develop a plan to reach a goal. Unable to break down into small, reachable steps, whether it be spiritual, relational, financial, emotional, or sexual.
Judgment	Lacks judgment in important daily decision-making. Impulsivity and poor judgment, traits that often accompany ADD, strain a relationship.

IMPULSIVE ARE WE

For most people, there are a few vital nanoseconds between stimulus and response that cause them to say to themselves, *Just because someone has twenty items in the fifteen-item lane doesn't mean I have to start a verbal disturbance at Checkout 7. There are saner ways of handling this minor annoyance . . . like moving to Checkout 6, perhaps.* But this all-important "thinking gap" doesn't work as well with ADD types. So, frankly, they end up mopping up many negative consequences that go with unchecked impulsivity. Quite often their feeling and reaction center in their brain starts firing before their logic and reason center kicks in. And this explains why the majority of prisoners and addiction-prone people also have ADD. (Most men with porn addictions have an ADD component. Because the area of sexual addiction is such a large and painful issue in marriage, I am devoting a special appendix to and for couples dealing with this problem. Brain science is offering new hope for those struggling to break this particularly devastating addiction.)

A tendency toward impulsivity, however, also explains why ADDers are often as lovable as puppies. They tend to be less inhibited when showing or expressing deep, genuine feelings of tenderness and affection in spontaneous moments. This adorability factor is a lifesaving trait, because if ADD types didn't have it, many people would wring their necks in abject frustration.

Does the lovability factor mean scattered types are excused from their wrongdoings? No. But does it mean that they may have less willpower and control than another person whose PFC is functioning beautifully? Yes. Should we have a little more compassion and patience toward people whose brains are not firing properly? I believe so.

In fact, once I can show a husband or wife that his or her mate's brain is literally functioning without the normal *Pause* button, compassion rises accordingly. Also, there's a sense of relief that passes over the man and woman who have no idea why they've struggled so much to be good, or on time, or neat, or organized, or able to sit and listen with interest to the ones they love. They realize that their battle to cooperate within societal norms or expectations is tougher than it is for many others.

"But," I can hear someone asking, "why was my partner all ears when we were dating? Why was he *so* attentive to me, hanging on my every word? Where did all that attention go once we tied the knot?"

The answer to that puzzling question, too, can be found through SPECT imaging studies. Many assume that people with ADD cannot focus, that they are always scattered. However, it is probably more accurate to say that the issue is not one of lack of focus: it is actually *overfocus*—on something novel, curious, distracting, or of very high interest. That focus may happen to be on a new girlfriend or boyfriend or the interesting fly that just landed on the windowsill.

You may have heard Eastern writers refer to a mind that jumps around all the time as a "monkey mind." Imagine that your inner Curious George never took a nap. In some ways, being married to a person with ADD is not unlike taking a walk in nature with a curious toddler with all the wondering and wandering that goes with such an adventure. "What's on that leaf?" "Why does that worm have a sweater on?" "Can I throw this rock in the water?" "What would happen if I put this stick in that knothole?" "I want to taste that berry!" "Let's stop here. No, let's go over there! Wait! What's that sound?" In the same way that toddlers exasperate a mom on a mission—like getting to the end of the block—and simultaneously inspire grins and tender love and even admiration, so do most ADD types who bounce or meander into my office (with their head-shaking mates giving me desperate looks, nonverbal pleas for help, as they either follow or lead their spouses into the room).

Though this may not be pleasant to hear, when you two were brand-new and novel, your ADD lover was all eyes and ears with total attention on you. But as he became "more accustomed to your face," his brain had more trouble with focusing on the familiar. That would be *you*. I know: *Ouch.*

This is why I often hear, "Dr. Henslin, in order to get my husband's attention, I practically have to hang from a tree in a clown costume!" Or, sadly, "The only way to get my lover to focus on me is to shake him up in some way—threaten to leave him, blow up at him, pretend I'm interested in someone else. Then I suddenly become the object of his pursuit. But I'm exhausted from this game of trying to 'get Chris's attention.' Surely there is an easier way!"

And this is where I love being able to share the good news. "Yes! There is an easier way. There's help! I'm so glad you are both here!"

FOCUSING SOUP FOR THE SCATTERED SOUL

Once we are sure that a mate has ADD or ADHD and have narrowed down the particular type of ADD, there is a wide variety of ways we can help. Often just a little bit of medication can prove miraculous. Stimulants such as Adderall or Ritalin are fairly easy to try, should a doctor advise you to try a sample, because the results are almost immediate, and the drug also wears off in a few hours. It sounds odd that a stimulant would help with focusing and hyperactivity problems. But actually it makes sense. Stimulant medication helps bring the blood flow to where it is needed most in the PFC and increases focus.

People with milder forms of ADD may be helped by supplements that increase focus. Among the most popular of these is an amino acid called tyrosine, but you can also find a combination of supplements at your health food store or through the Amen Clinic that include a variety of amino acids that are specifically designed to help create a sense of calm and focus. Ginkgo is another herb that helps with mental clarity, memory, and focus. High-quality fish oil has also proven to be of tremendous help with people who have ADD. It literally lubricates and nourishes brain tissues and has profoundly good results on balancing mood and hyperactivity in kids and adults.

Dr. Amen is one of the world's most renowned experts in ADD and through SPECT imaging research has identified six subtypes of this common imbalance. It is estimated that 10 percent of the population struggles with some form of ADD, and as time and research marches on, even the staunchest naysayers in the scientific community have a hard time arguing with the brain-scan realities. Each subtype needs a specialized treatment, and in some cases, the typical prescription for Adderall or Ritalin can actually make things worse. That's why it is important to determine the exact type of ADD that you or your mate may have. (You can take an online test through the Amen Clinic's Web site for a nominal charge—around five dollars—or read Dr. Amen's detailed and helpful book, *Healing ADD*.)

The chart that follows lists the kinds of ADD that Dr. Amen has isolated. I've listed areas where a person may need improvement and my recommendation for strategies that have proven helpful to me and my clients:

Subtype	Areas for Growth	Strategies
Classic ADD	Great beginnings and poor follow-through. Impulsive decisions that do not have long-term goals in mind. Saying everything on your mind.	Find out the supplement and/or medication strategy that helps build healthy neurochemistry. A spouse who is naturally organized can be very helpful to you, as long as there's a spirit of kindness between you. If you give your mate permission to help, he or she can remind you of deadlines and help you with the next right step when you feel overwhelmed. Learn to find joy in completion and the creation of order. Think of organization as "being kind to your future self." You are cleaning your desk now as an act of graciousness to yourself tomorrow! Some sense of structure will actually help create and implement greater and better creative ideas. If you say something impulsive that is hurtful, apologize as soon as possible and work to not repeat that mistake.
Inattentive	Easily distracted. Jump from project to project. Tendency to jump to conclusions without really hearing partners fully and deeply.	Develop appropriate supplement and/or medication to help prefrontal function so as not to sabotage self or marriage. Taking notes as your mate is talking to track what is being said may be a helpful thing to do when your mate really needs you to be attentive. Create a system, together, that keeps you on top of your tasks or daily duties at home.
Overfocused	Find yourself being perfectionistic with details. Holding on to grudges and resentments. Argumentative and/or oppositional in relationships. Black-and-white thinking. "My way or the highway."	Develop appropriate supplement and/or medication to help cingulate function or the part of the brain that gets stuck on a looping thought. Read books on forgiveness, and grow in compassion, kindness, and spirituality. Take active steps toward letting go. Resentment that is one day old is hurting you more than the person you are angry with. Become self-aware of your mind becoming oppositional or argumentative. Remember, the angst could be stemming from overactivity in your cingulate, rather than the issue at hand. Ask yourself the question inside before responding: *Are my thoughts and what I'm planning to say going to bring me closer to my mate or create distance?* When you automatically become black-and-white on issues, you are not using your powers of creativity. Usually there is a third way, a win-win that one or both of you are not yet seeing.

Subtype	Areas for Growth	Strategies
Temporal Lobe	Become easily volatile. Quick reactions rather than responding. Overreaction to facial expressions or tone of voice.	It is crucial to get effective treatment for temporal lobe problems. If you are taking medication, know how long it stays in your system. If you are overreacting, see if it is near the time when you need your next dose of medication. If you are married to someone who has temporal lobe problems, you'll need to master some coping strategies. For example, the moment he or she begins to overreact, calmly say, "For the sake of our relationship, I will talk with you in about an hour." Set the boundary, turn, and walk away. It generally takes one hour, if the person is not obsessing on the issue, to be able to calm down and talk rationally without exploding.
Limbic	In addition to lack of focus, can be prone to depression and feelings of hopelessness. Struggles to be optimistic during difficult times. Will bring mood of the marriage down. Family members of this ADD may describe themselves as feeling as though they are living with a black cloud.	First make sure good nutrition and exercise are in place on a daily basis as a priority. Then, deal with ANTS (automatic negative thoughts) and replace them with a more joyful way of seeing the world. If still struggling, try supplements and/or medication as listed on the following pages. The right combination of all of the above should bring much needed relief to both the depressed spouse and his or her mate.
Ring of Fire	Can become quickly volatile, just like the temporal lobe subtype. May be more manipulative, and will play one person against the other. You seek relationships that are calming and then become irritable if a person is not always "there" for you. May be inconsistent in your version of the truth, depending on who you are talking to and your feelings at the time. May go from job to job. Tend to make a lot of excuses. Tend to create chaos, crisis, and drama in relationships.	This is one of the most difficult types to treat because it requires careful attention to medication; otherwise your manipulative and controlling behaviors kick in, in order to manage your increasing internal anxiety. It is difficult for you to seek help and benefit from counseling because self-confrontation is so difficult. You often are "frozen" in your emotional development, quickly placing blame on others, and have difficulty seeing your own role in problems. Because you tend to pit one family member against another, it is helpful for family members to talk and create a unified front and clear boundaries.

SPECT SCAN OF ADD BEFORE AND AFTER TREATMENT

The SPECT scans that follow are called *surface scans*. They measure the blood flow, or perfusion, in a brain. You'll note that in the pictures on the left, it looks as though there are a couple of holes in the front of the brain, in the PFC. These are not actual holes but are places that are lacking in good blood flow. Note the improvement in the second set of scans, after receiving medication to help bring more blood to the front of the brain. Beautiful!

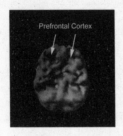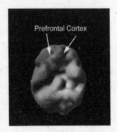

ADD surface scans, before and after treatment

SIX SUBTYPES OF ADD

Here again are the six different types of ADD, each with different brain function issues and treatment protocols:

Type 1: Classic ADD

   Symptoms: primary ADD symptoms plus hyperactivity, restlessness, and impulsivity

   SPECT: usually low prefrontal cortex with concentration

   Supplements: multiple vitamin, NeuroEPA fish oil, L-tyrosine or DL-phenylalanine

   Medications: stimulant medications, such as Adderall, Concerta, Ritalin, or Dexedrine

Type 2: Inattentive ADD

   Symptoms: primary ADD symptoms plus low energy and motivation, spacey, and internally preoccupied. Type 2 is diagnosed later in life, if at all.

It is more common in girls. These are quiet kids and adults, often labeled lazy, unmotivated, and not that smart.

SPECT: usually low prefrontal cortex with concentration and low cerebral activity

Supplements: multiple vitamin, NeuroEPA fish oil, L-tyrosine or DL-phenylalanine

Medications: stimulant medications, such as Adderall, Concerta, Ritalin, or Dexedrine

Type 3: Overfocused ADD

Symptoms: primary ADD symptoms plus cognitive inflexibility, trouble shifting attention, stuck on negative thoughts or behaviors, worrying, holding grudges, argumentative, oppositional, and a need for sameness; often seen in families with addiction problems or obsessive-compulsive tendencies

SPECT: usually high anterior cingulate activity plus low prefrontal cortex with concentration

Supplements: multiple vitamin, NeurOmega fish oil, 5-HTP, L-tryptophan or St. John's wort plus L-tyrosine

Medications: antidepressant Effexor or a combination of an SSRI, like Prozac and a stimulant

Type 4: Temporal Lobe ADD

Symptoms: primary ADD symptoms plus a short fuse; misinterprets comments, periods of anxiety, headaches, or abdominal pain; history of head injury; family history of rages, dark thoughts, memory problems, or struggles with reading; often seen in families with learning or temper problems

SPECT: usually low temporal lobe activity plus low prefrontal cortex with concentration

Supplements: multiple vitamin, high-quality fish oil, GABA or taurine for irritability, or Brain Vitale or NeuroMemory (available from the Amen Clinic) for memory issues

Medications: by themselves, stimulants such as Adderall or Ritalin usually make people with this type more irritable; effectively treated with a combination of antiseizure medications (such as Neurontin) and stimulants

Type 5: Limbic ADD

Symptoms: primary ADD symptoms plus chronic mild sadness, negativity, low energy, low self-esteem, irritability, social isolation, and poor appetite and sleep patterns. Stimulants, by themselves, usually cause problems with rebound or cause depressive symptoms.

SPECT: usually high deep limbic activity plus low prefrontal cortex at rest and with concentration

Supplements: multiple vitamin, NeurOmega fish oil, SAM-e or DL-phenylalanine

Medications: stimulating antidepressants, such as Wellbutrin

Type 6: Ring of Fire ADD

Symptoms: primary ADD symptoms plus extreme moodiness, anger outbursts, oppositional, inflexibility, fast thoughts, excessive talking, and very sensitive to sounds and lights. I named it Ring of Fire after the intense ring of overactivity that I saw in the brains of affected people. This type is usually made much worse by stimulants.

SPECT: marked overall increased activity across the cortex; may or may not have low prefrontal cortex activity

Supplements: multiple vitamin, NeurOmega fish oil, NeuroLink (contains 5-HTP, GABA, and L-tyrosine)

Medications: anticonvulsants (such as Neurontin) and SSRI medication or novel antipsychotic medications (such as Risperdal or Zyprexa)

ADD IN THE BEDROOM

Intimacy with an ADD partner presents its own challenges, so I am going to devote a little time and space to talk about that here. Many ADD types need a little time to disengage from the activity at hand to refocus on lovemaking. First, disconnect from the TV or computer. Consider taking a hot bath (try lavender-scented Epsom salts or bubble bath); light an aromatherapy candle (in your favorite romantic scent); turn on some sensual music; begin directing your thoughts toward your beloved and loving him or her sensually.

Focus on memories of when you fell in love, your first kiss, and your past wonderful lovemaking experiences.

Remember, men: with no forethought there is no foreplay. Sometimes men do not make the connection that foreplay is all of life outside of the bedroom. When the frontal cortex is working great, you will evidence forethought or, in other words, you will think things through before you say them or do them. A misspoken word or unkind behavior will wipe out sexual desire. Your wife can be having thoughts of wanting to make love and be feeling hot toward you and, unfortunately, your behavior can sabotage that moment.

On the other hand, because I have so often observed that a scattered personality type marries a hyperfocused personality, I also look at the possibility that there are two brain issues clashing in the bedroom. In the next chapter we'll talk about people who are overfocused and often get stuck in things having to be their way. These spouses tend to look for reasons not to make love, saying an automatic no to lovemaking more than saying yes. When a spouse says things like "I can live without sex," or "Sex is not that important in our relationship"—especially to an ADD partner—despair may set in. Exercise and a healthy sex life are two of the best brain balancers for Scattered Lovers. So try hard to focus on the good things your ADD spouse is doing, put aside small irritations, and give both of yourselves the balm of lovemaking as often as possible. The professional baseball player who consistently hits over .300 will make millions, but a husband who bats .800 in all that he does may still strike out in bed if his wife has unresolved issues with relaxing and going with the sensual flow. For these wives I recommend they mentally put a bumper sticker on their bed that says, "Just Say Yes. You'll Probably Have *Fun!*"

On the other hand, many Scattered Lover types may tend to make their partners feel like objects to satisfy their own need for sex, using their mates as medication to calm them down. They take the shortcut around foreplay because they are overfocused on getting to the main event. To practice slowing down and savoring lovemaking, it is very helpful to practice giving each other slow and sensual massages or loving touches, with zero expectation of climaxing. Sex therapists call this *sensate focusing*. In the Song of Solomon the couple savors each other. The man loves every inch of his wife's body, taking time to learn and sense what pleasures his wife the most. If he is inattentive or hyperactive out of the bed, ladies, most likely he will be the same way in bed. In his fantasy, since he is having fun, he assumes his wife is also having a wondrous experience, while in reality each lovemaking session could feel like an exercise in emptiness and frustration to her. Women tend to need a longer time to warm up and orgasm.

Conway Twitty and the Pointer Sisters both extolled the virtues of s-l-o-w-ing down in the bedroom, with the classic song "Slow Hand." If you've not heard it, go to www.youtube.com and type in the song's title and either "Pointer Sisters" or "Conway Twitty," depending on whether you prefer pop or country. It's like sex therapy in a song for people who need to learn the pleasures of taking it easy. Listen to it and replay it as often as you need to before making love as a reminder to stop being in such a hurry, to savor your mate and your intimate time together. If you are a two-minute lover and she isn't looking dreamily into your eyes after lovemaking, wanting to cuddle and be close . . . start that escrow account for marital therapy now. Believe me, you will need it!

Take responsibility to bring your best brain to the marriage bed by doing whatever it takes—seeing a doctor, reading or listening to the suggested books at the end of this chapter, seeing a marriage coach who specializes in ADD clients—to become the most loving partner you can be.

Remember that having ADD is not your fault, but it is 100 percent *your* responsibility to deal with it.

Here are some ways that scattered-types can begin bringing their best brain to the table of marriage.

TEN TIPS FOR A SCATTERED LOVER TO INCREASE FOCUS

1. *Use food to help focus.*

Protein at every meal, even mini-meals and snacks, will help keep focus sharp. Try to save most carbs for the evening hours when you are ready to relax. Many people find that eliminating sugar or wheat and preservatives helps them with calm and focus.

2. Go fish!

Adults should take 2,000–4,000 mg of high-quality fish oil a day (1,000–2000 mg for children). For types 1 and 2, NeuroEPA from the Amen Clinics is a high-quality brand. For types 3 to 6, NeurOmega is best. For children or adults who have problems digesting fish oil, check out the Coromega product: a fish oil that tastes like orange pudding with no fishy aftertaste. In fact, as more is known about the powerful and positive effects of fish oil, more manufacturers are finding ways to make it more palatable to the public—including putting it in chocolate. Some people find that the lemon-flavored fish oil capsules (such as Natrol, available at Walgreens) or enteric-coated capsules (which often smell like vanilla) do not produce "fish burps."

Also try to eliminate caffeine from your diet. It interferes with sleep and the other treatments. Your nutritional supplements and high-quality diet will give you the energy you need without side effects or experiencing a nervous high that soon bottoms out and crashes.

L-tyrosine is often helpful to wake up sleepy brains. There are several good "focusing" supplements on the market, such as True Focus by NOW with amino acids, like L-tyrosine and DPLA, along with other supportive herbs and vitamins.

3. Get intense aerobic exercise for thirty to forty-five minutes daily.

Long, fast walks will help burn off excess energy. If sitting still is difficult for you, pass up invitations to long dinners and opt to go for a walk or play tennis with friends instead. Become aware of your own need for preventive self-care. If you anticipate that being stuck in a long social situation is going to leave you irritable or antsy, let your spouse know that you'll need a walk midway through the evening to discharge some energy.

4. Avoid distractions.

Set up a corner in your house that is totally free from noise and windows to get your paperwork completed. One friend of mine goes to the local corner bakery during the nonbusy hours to write and work without distractions that come with being at home. Many cafés and coffee shops have free Wi-Fi (wireless local network) and can be nice alternative "offices" if there are too many distractions at home for you to get computer or writing work done.

5. Be willing to consider medication, if diet, supplements, and coping strategies aren't working.

A word of warning: note that the last three subtypes of ADD, all with a tendency toward anger or irritability, can be made worse by stimulants such as Adderall and Ritalin. If you have issues with hair-trigger or explosive temper, you will want to either get a brain scan or use particular caution when trying a stimulant. In these cases we always try to make sure the temporal lobes are calmed first before addressing any ADD issues. Bringing the above list in to your physician could be helpful. Or call our office for recommendations.

6. Get creative with self-help.

Keep a stack of legal pads and pens at your bedside and make a to-do list each morning to keep yourself on track for the day.

Give yourself a lot of margin—extra time to get ready and go where you must be.

If you find yourself avoiding chores and neglecting duties, stop and think about them. Ask yourself if there is a more creative or fun way to tackle boring, routine responsibilities. You can do this by attaching a little reward to the mundane: Take out the trash and stop to shoot some basketballs on the way back into the house. Turn on your favorite music to wash dishes by. Make a game out of work; set the timer and see how fast you can make the bed or clean the bathroom. Save laundry to fold while watching a favorite TV show. Put some fun in your function!

7. Allow time to recharge your batteries between activities.

This varies for everyone. Some ADD types enjoy a nap or a hot bath; some prefer a hard walk or a game of driveway basketball. No matter your preference for discharging stress, leave margin in your life for recharging your brain's "batteries."

8. Limit TV, video games, and time at the computer.

It is hard for people with ADD to disengage from these mentally stimulating activities in order to engage with their mates. So predetermine a set length of time to watch TV, play games, and answer e-mail. Using a timer to help when it's time to switch to another activity is helpful. A warning bell that signals time will be up in five minutes helps an ADD person to begin the transition of ending one activity to engage in the next.

9. *Notice when your best "focused time" is . . .*

. . . and use these times for significant conversations with your mate or your boss. If you know that you are easily distracted and get overloaded, keep the discussion short and focused but promise to follow up with another discussion time when you are able to be clear and tune in. Best focus times vary for ADD types, but most find they are most fully awake and aware after they've had their medication or eaten a healthy meal and had a good night's sleep.

10. *Strategize ways to be on time.*

If you tend to be late, put clocks *everywhere* in the house—that means in every room. (You can find little ones at the dollar store.) Give yourself a margin of extra time to allow for any lollygagging, or forgetting, or meandering time. Use your cell phone to manage yourself. Set one of the alarms on your phone to go off when you need to leave to be on time for your appointments—especially for date night with your spouse. Make a commitment to drop everything when that alarm goes off. Develop a history of being there five minutes early rather than routinely five to ten minutes or one hour . . . or one day later! (Many people believe I will be late for my own funeral. When I die and they call me the "late" Earl Henslin, they'll be referring to the memory of how I struggled with being on time.) Put a hook by the front door, and train yourself to put your keys or purse in the same place every time you walk in until it becomes an automatic behavior.

TEN TIPS TO HELP FOCUS YOUR SCATTERED MATE

Be sure to read the advice directed to the ADD partner and ponder how you might be supportive in his or her efforts to implement some of the coping strategies. Now here's a bit of encouragement and advice for you.

1. *Dr. Amen emphasizes that in dealing with kids, employees, and spouses who have ADD—NO YELLING.*

On his Web site he writes:

Many people with ADD seek conflict or excitement as a means of
stimulation. They can be masters at making other people mad or
angry (and often enjoy playing the mental/relational game called
"Let's Have a Problem"). Do not lose your temper with them. If they
get you to explode, their unconscious, low-energy prefrontal cortex
lights up and likes it. Never let your anger be their medication. They
can get addicted to it.[3]

2. *Accept what cannot be changed, and work around it.*

A very patient friend of mine is married to a scattered wife. She's not
hyper in body, but her mind is always flitting about from one thing to another.
When, after much trial and error, he could not keep her from absentmindedly
throwing away the lids to the milk carton, and he didn't want his dairy tasting
like yesterday's tuna fish, he came up with a solution. He began collecting
milk lids and putting them in a drawer. When she lost a lid, absently tossing
it away, he simply and quietly replaced it from his "lid stash."

3. *Remember: your mate isn't doing this on purpose.*

Perhaps the most common complaint from spouses is that their mates
rarely finish chores or complete projects. It helps to remember that your
spouse is not being lazy or insensitive. Most adults with ADD or ADHD
have to expend an enormous amount of energy to maintain focus at work
and stifle their tendencies to wander. Many tend to come home and collapse,
in dire need of recharging their brains. They really do need time to recuperate
between requirements for focusing. Here's some advice from those who have
loved and lived with a Scattered Lover:

- Don't take it personally.
- Get him started or work alongside him to get chores done.
- Help him create systems that become no-brainers. Have a box by
  the door to catch muddy shoes and a coat tree for coats and hats.
  A central message board in the kitchen with pushpins and cork can
  be handy.

- Post a to-do schedule, and try to keep it consistent. For example:
  - ✓ Do laundry on Sunday evening.
  - ✓ Buy groceries on Tuesdays.
  - ✓ Pay bills on the 1st and 15th.
- Better yet, get a big, easy-to-read calendar and write in weekly or monthly reminders.

4. Minimize the difficulty of tasks, and offer moral support.

Scattered Lovers have a tendency to agree to do something and neglect the follow-through for a variety of reasons. Sometimes their mouths go into autopilot—"Yes, dear"—while their brains are somewhere else completely. They really and truly will not recall that you asked them to do something, and they agreed. Talk about irritating! Other times, something on the to-do list just seems overwhelming.

My wife, Karen, once asked me to fix the back gate. I avoided the gate like the plague, imagining a huge, complicated task, involving seven trips to Home Depot because, though I'm a great therapist, a handyman I am not. One day when I came home from work, I knew I was in trouble. Karen met me with eyes that were *not* happy. Apparently our dog, Sparky, whose main tricks were breathing and wagging his tail, had wandered through the broken open gate, down the street, and through the door of a neighbor's house, where he proceeded to leave a "present" on our neighbor's kitchen floor.

Newly motivated, I quickly went to look at the gate. (ADD people will get things done with a crisis or deadline.) Turned out, it was a small issue, a loose screw, and I had it fixed in no time.

What could have helped motivate me to fix the gate weeks earlier? Perhaps Karen could have gone with me and helped assess the damage and cure together. Maybe a trip to the hardware store could have turned into a Saturday date with a stop for a treat on the way home (Will Fix Gates for Ice-Cream Shop Stop). Anything a mate can do to minimize the difficulty of a task and help us get started—even if it is just standing by for moral support—is very helpful. ADD types need a lot of cheering on.

5. Stop doing what isn't working.

If you are irritated by something that isn't being done by your mate, make your request clear. If the action is not taken, either do it yourself, pay to have it done, or barter with someone else to get it done. You need to know that nagging, coercing, whining, intimidating, threatening, yelling, and throwing a fit are all strategies that will not work.

6. Positive reinforcement works best.

Catch them being good, and praise the heck out of them. Try saying something like, "Honey, see that trash can there? When it is emptied, I have a big kiss waiting for my big, strong man." Yes, it's cheesy. But most guys will still fall for that line every time. We're all basically still little boys ready to prove our manliness to the adoring girls in this world.

7. Ignore behaviors that aren't worth the hassle.

Let as many small irritations go as you possibly can. Pick your battles. Focus more on what you love about them than their disorganization.

8. Think like an animal trainer.

Use a kind tone of voice and gentle gestures along with plenty of humor to defuse difficult situations. It helps to think more like an animal trainer when "training your spouse" to do certain things. This may sound demeaning, but it is so much more fun and effective than nagging (check out my list of "Good Reads" for more insight on this, especially the Amy Sutherland book).

9. Don't blame yourself for being unable to micromanage your spouse.

You can be helpful and supportive, but ultimately your mate must take 100 percent responsibility to balance her own brain. You can take 100 percent responsibility for your response to her and how to become a bit wiser and more ADD savvy. But you'll need a lot of support and encouragement.

10. Create environments to lessen stress and upsize your mate's success.

If, for example, you know your mate isn't skilled or thrilled about cleaning house and you can afford a maid, by all means, hire one. If you can't, then do what you can to help create a low-maintenance house. Keep a minimalist look, without a lot of gadgets and knickknacks; find carpets and countertops in colors that don't need constant upkeep to look clean. Use disposable cleaning wipes in the kitchen and bathroom to make quick, easy work of cleaning up. Spend a weekend with your mate, working alongside each other to cut your stuff in half—by giving it away or throwing it away or selling it on eBay.

Good Reads to Encourage the Scattered Soul
(and the Spouse Who Lives with Said Soul)

- *Is It You, Me, or Adult A.D.D.? Stopping the Roller Coaster When Someone You Love Has Attention Deficit Disorder* by Gina Pera
- *What Shamu Taught Me About Life, Love, and Marriage: Lessons for People from Animals and Their Trainers* by Amy Sutherland (or read the author's June 2006 *New York Times* article that prompted the book at: www.nytimes.com/2006/06/25/fashion/25love.html?ei=5070)
- *ADD in Intimate Relationships* by Dr. Daniel Amen
- *Healing ADD* by Dr. Daniel Amen
- *Getting Through to the Man You Love: The No-Nonsense, No-Nagging Guide for Women* by Michele Weiner-Davis (All of Michele Weiner-Davis's books are solution-focused, a strategy that works very well with a spouse who may be a little ADD. This book is full of practical ideas to redirect a spouse without yelling or nagging.)
- Dr. Amen's books and other excellent resources, including online testing and DVDs, can be found at www.amenclinics.com; click "Online store."

REMEMBER THE MAGIC IN THEIR MESS

Becky Johnson, who is the collaborator for this book, also struggles with inattentive ADD. (Yes, it is a miracle we can get a whole book written together.

But remember, when we are involved in something interesting—like writing this book—we can focus like crazy.) The same for Becky's sister, Rachel St. John Gilbert. Both sisters have made a career out of writing, speaking, and telling funny stories about their mishaps. They both married calm, focused, highly organized men who are sympathetic to their brain limitations and deeply supportive of their creative bents.

Becky received an e-mail from her sister this week, summing up a typical day in the life of a creative family. Some background: Rachel's son, Trevor, has the lead in this year's high-school play, *Man of La Mancha,* and will likely go on to a career in acting; her daughter Tori, at age seven, makes her stage debut in community theater this year. The youngest child, Whitney (age 5), can usually be found traipsing around in the costume of the day, which could be anything from wearing her mother's nightie, as if it were a fairy princess gown, or sporting a bucket on her head as she imitates a robot. Walking into their home is like walking backstage at a Broadway play, with one kid practicing his lines and another belting out show tunes like a mini Ethel Merman, the other tearing through a closet in search of a cape. The stack of CDs in their car stereo reads like a who's who of America's Best Loved Musicals.

Enough backdrop. Now to the e-mail from Rachel to Becky:

OK, Becky, I can't find my keys or my head most of the time. But the other morning Tori was having a hard time getting up and getting her shower. So she asks, "What time is it?" and I say, "It's 7:16 going on 17," and then . . . It was magic. Right in the bathroom, I grabbed her and began ballroom dancing (as best I could with the toilet in the way . . .) and sang, à la the romantic, a rain-soaked scene from the Sound of Music: *"It is sixteen going on seventeen . . . you have to get all clean! You can't be late, 'cause Ms. Baldwin hates it, when you are late for schooooool." Then we both collapsed in a big laugh. It was pretty wonderful. So yeah, what if I am lacking in organizational skills? What if it is a struggle every single day to get myself and the kids in the car on time? I can do a mean Julie Andrews any time I want. And my kids are gonna be* stars, *baby!*

Alas, Scattered Lovers may step on your last nerve. But at least they often do it with top hat and tap shoes and a smile to beat the band.

Trying to see the best in their personalities, applauding them when they do well, and giving them an understanding hug and a helping hand when they are overwhelmed, will endear us to those scattered spouses we've vowed to love for life. And at least we will never be bored.

Please rate yourself on each of the symptoms listed below, using the following scale:

0=Never 1=Rarely 2=Occasionally 3=Frequently 4=Very Frequently
N/A=Not Applicable/Not Known
(You answer in one column, your mate in the other column.)

____ ____ 1. Excessive or senseless worrying

____ ____ 2. Upset when things do not go your way

____ ____ 3. Upset when things are out of place

____ ____ 4. Tendency to be oppositional or argumentative

____ ____ 5. Tendency to have repetitive negative thoughts

____ ____ 6. Tendency toward compulsive behaviors

____ ____ 7. Intense dislike for change

____ ____ 8. Tendency to hold grudges

____ ____ 9. Trouble shifting attention from subject to subject

____ ____ 10. Trouble shifting behavior from task to task

____ ____ 11. Difficulties seeing options in situations

____ ____ 12. Tendency to hold on to own opinion and not listen to others

____ ____ 13. Tendency to get locked into a course of action, whether or not it is good

____ ____ 14. Needing to have things done a certain way or you become very upset

____ ____ 15. Complaints from others that you worry too much

____ ____ 16. Tendency to say no without first thinking about question

____ ____ 17. Tendency to predict fear

Results: If five or more symptoms are rated 3 or 4, there's a high probability that the SPECT scan will show an overactive cingulate gyrus.

From Amen Brain Subsystem Checklist, used by permission from Dr. Daniel Amen and the Amen Clinic.

CHAPTER FIVE

The Overfocused Lover
(Cingulate Gyrus)

Love does not dominate; it cultivates.

—GOETHE

After a time of laughing together at the latest comedy release, Bob and Connie walked out of the theater, arm in arm, into a beautiful evening. They decided to enjoy a leisurely dinner at their favorite restaurant, then walk slowly along the river boardwalk. Prior to this evening, they'd both had difficult weeks. Bob had been out of town much of the week, involved in high-pressure business negotiations. Connie had to care for both children alone. One morning she woke up to a soaking wet carpet, the result of a toilet overflowing all night long as she and the kids slept in ignorant bliss. Three days later, after a parade of plumbers, rented and borrowed fans, and help from friends, the smells were finally gone, and the carpet was usable again.

Their daughter, who had learning disabilities, needed two to three hours of help with her homework each night, so Connie welcomed a break from the endless routine of caring for the kids. She'd looked forward to this evening out with her husband to reconnect all day. She had missed Bob and during dinner listened to all the victories of his business trip with pride. As they were walking, she began to share with him about what her tough week had been like.

Bob, however, had nothing on his mind at this point but thoughts of relaxing and making love—hopefully as soon as they walked in the door. In fact, he'd been able to think of little else during the last part of their long week apart. And now, as she droned on about the carpet and the kids, all he could hear was the sound of a Honey-Do Agenda in her voice, which signaled one thing to him: no sex tonight. Blinded by his own disappointment in what he perceived she was actually saying, he totally missed her intention. He tensed up, dropped her hand, and said something terse.

The truth is that Connie was actually sharing her heart with her husband and giving him an "emotional bid"—a signal for him to draw closer to her, to connect with her hurt, and to listen, tend, and soothe her heart as a preparation for lovemaking. Like most women, she desperately needed him to tend to her heart before she could lovingly relax and give him her body. But Bob had made up his mind: "She doesn't want me"—and from past experience, Connie knew that there was nothing she could say or do to persuade him otherwise once he was convinced of his own version of the truth. In fact, when he got a negative thought in his head, it was like a runaway train. All hopes for intimacy were gone, and just to keep a modicum of peace, Connie shut down, got quiet, and avoided her husband's flashing eyes and agitated murmurings.

Inside, Connie felt her muscles tense, and whatever romantic thoughts and feelings had been there vanished into the warm spring evening. When they walked in the door of their home, Connie quietly retreated upstairs to a hot bubble bath and a book, followed by the warmth and comfort of a soft bed. She let the tears fall into her pillow, alone. Bob went to his computer in the study and, under the auspices of checking his e-mail, gave in to his pent-up lust while staring at the visual image of an artificial woman who would not require anything of him that he wasn't up to giving.

WHAT HAPPENS WHEN THE CINGULATE IS OVERACTIVE?

Neither Bob nor Connie began their romantic evening out with thoughts that they'd end up sleeping in separate rooms, experiencing that depth of loneliness that only married people who are not connecting can know. This night was not an isolated incident, but one that transpired too often. It had become their "Repeat Fight"—you know, the fight in a marriage that never really goes away; it just comes back in slightly different versions. Connie felt that she could never compete with the negative version of her voice in Bob's head, and eventually grew hopeless. She stopped trying to argue with him because it turned out to be a waste of emotional energy. She was growing numb inside, having to construct a cocoonlike boundary to keep from anymore hurt. Her growing apathy toward Bob frightened her, as it did Bob, and it wasn't long before they came to see me.

After the intake, I got Bob to agree to a SPECT scan, and it showed that an area of his brain, called the cingulate gyrus, which runs across the middle of the brain (from front to back) was lit up and overactive. The cingulate, when working well, helps us shift from thought to thought, let go of negativity, stay open to new interpretations, and generally go with the flow. When it is overactive, it is like a gerbil on a wheel. The negative thoughts go round and round, over and over the same territory.

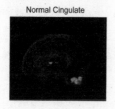
Normal Cingulate

Overactive Cingulate

In Bob's scan, we see a brain that is so easily irritated and angered that the people around him are almost guaranteed to be walking on eggshells.

Let's take a look at this next chart and see the difference between a healthy and an overactive cingulate.

Healthy Cingulate	Overactive Cingulate
Flexible; able to move from one thought to another.	Black-and-white thinking.
When experiencing a wrong done against you, you are able to forgive and let go.	Will store hurts, angers, and resentments. Have difficulty forgiving and moving on. In conflict, will bring up hurts, anger, and resentments from years ago.
Able to see positive and hold on to it.	Will notice everything that is wrong in a relationship; have difficulty seeing the positive.
Able to create order in environment, but disorder does not cause anger or fear.	Can be compulsive about order and cleaning. Upset if anything is left out or system of order is disrupted.

Healthy Cingulate	Overactive Cingulate
When a negative or self-critical thought enters the mind, able to refocus on positive.	Unable to let go of negative or self-critical thoughts; will replay them over and over in the mind, which can increase anger, hurt, or fears. Actually will rehearse negative thoughts about spouse and will play a role in the relationship's deteriorating.
Allow mind to see options.	Tunnel vision; will see limited options, which will make for difficulty in conflict resolution. "My way or the highway." "Agree to disagree" is not an option. Use overcontrolling behaviors to relieve personal anxiety; often unaware that methods are harming the potential for intimacy in the marriage.
Comfortable with others having choices in the relationship.	Unless people in relationship make choices that meet expectations, will become upset; experienced as controlling in relationship.
Live more in present. Do not look at future with fear.	Tendency to predict gloom and doom when thinking about future events.

Let's take a little look at what a person with a hot cingulate is really feeling. The brain chemicals in this overfocused lover type get triggered by something in his environment that makes him feel oddly anxious. In Bob's case, it was the perception, however wrong, that his wife was making a complaint list in order to avoid his advances. Perhaps this had really happened in one incident years ago, and Bob had never let go of this memory. This thought made Bob feel stressed, and under stress, a person with an overactive cingulate latches on to the first anxious thought and cannot release it. It runs through his brain again and again, like the aforementioned gerbil on a wheel, and Lord help the person who tries to set the gerbil free. It ain't happening. Bob's on a one-way thought train that cannot be derailed.

One husband, whose wife had a "flaming cingulate" during PMS week, said, "I used to bang the phone on the counter to try to stop the ranting loop when my wife would call me, stuck on that gerbil wheel of negative thought. Nothing could shake her from her tirade of 'who done her wrong.'"

If you've ever offended or disappointed an overfocused lover, even if it was just a perceived offense, you've discovered that he can hold on to his grudges like a dog with a bone. Forgiving and letting go of real or perceived slights are among the most difficult things for a cingulate-minded person to do.

Yet it is amazing to watch what happens as people get this area of the brain calmed down. They retain all their formerly wonderful qualities but are simply calmer, more peaceful, and laid-back; they roll with the punches and go with the flow.

Until that oh-so-happy day, though, they will lean toward controlling behaviors as their only tool to self-medicate and calm inner anxiety. This could show itself in a number of ways. They could start micromanaging everyone around them, shouting orders or making random demands. They also may revert to super-organizing behaviors under stress: cleaning, doing laundry, even working on things like stamp collecting or putting a jigsaw puzzle together. There is a huge sense of satisfaction and relief when a controlling lover can find something—anything—to order, organize, or control. To the extreme this can lead to obsessive-compulsive–like disorders—hand-washing, counting things, or overchecking locks on doors. Sexual addictions may also occur because a man or woman can get locked on an image, followed by an impulse ("I have to do this!"). In fact, some sexual addiction counselors believe that porn addictions are, at the core, issues with control. A guy feels out of control, and here in cyberspace is someone, literally, "made to order." This power, as much as a sexual urge, calms the crazy-making gerbil in his brain.

We often see combinations of the cingulate with other mood problems in the brain. When people's cingulates *and* fear centers (basal ganglia) are overactive, an anxious thought can grow and become rampant, creating worst-case scenarios that cannot be redirected easily. If the cingulate and temporal lobes are overactive, they can get "stuck" on melancholy or raging thoughts. If the prefrontal cortex is not working well, as in cases of ADD with cingulate issues, there's nobody home to aid in impulse control, and addictions can have free rein with the brain. In fact, alcoholism and drug addiction are most common in people whose brain scans show this combination of low PFC and overactive cingulate.

Let me give you another example of a couple who were about to divorce because the man had cingulate issues that were out of control. Jordan was a top producer in his company, which is why businesses often put up with his random demands and controlling behaviors. Overfocused personalities can actually get a lot accomplished by sheer persistence and determination. But at home, this guy overcontrolled every penny in the house. And in Jordan's mind, he was simply being responsible, checking and rechecking their online bank balance several times every day.

Beside him in the counseling chair was his worn-out wife, Nathalie, who was also working and bringing in part of the family income. She was a smart, kind, and responsible person herself, but Jordan made her feel as though her paycheck belonged automatically to him. In fact, Nathalie said she felt like a child sent out to work all day long for a boss who simply whisked away all her earnings at the end of the day. Over time, her resentment and feelings of helplessness and frustration led her to ask for a divorce. Her view of their marriage reminded me of a sign I once saw:

> *My husband and I have religious differences.*
> *He thinks he's God, and I don't.*

This was, by the way, Jordan's second marriage. After hearing more about the first marriage, it became clear to me that he had also been super controlling in his first family and that it had probably led to outbursts of uncontrolled anger. He had been given very limited visitation rights with his children, and of course, this was all the "fault of the shoddy court system." (With this type, it always seems to be some other guy's fault.) Though he was trying to defend himself, the more he talked, the more I suspected a brain chemistry problem. And when I suspected it was a problem with the cingulate and perhaps also the temporal lobes (often indicated in men who rage), I braced myself for the inevitable debate.

After showing him some sample brain scans, I began describing what I suspected might be the cause of his compulsion to control (and trust me, I've learned to do this with as much tact and compassion as possible). Jordan looked up and said, "You are not a physician. Why are you talking to me about my brain? I came here for counseling. I'm not standing for this." Then he stood up and walked out in a huff. In the silence that filled the room in the man's absence, his wife looked at me and asked, "Now what am I going to do, Doc?"

I smiled compassionately and said, "Well, Nathalie, first I predict he'll blow again soon. It's not a question of whether he's going to be angry and controlling again; it is how soon and how angry. That's the way this kind of thing goes. You asked for my advice, and from my experience, this is what I suggest you do. When he blows up or tries to control you again, just tell him, 'Jordan, you need to go back and see Dr. Henslin and get a scan, or I am leaving. It's over.'"

I assured her that without her forcing a crisis, her husband would never get help. If she waited any longer, her love for him would fade so much that she would not want him back no matter what he did. In cases such as this, the earlier the belittled spouse forces a crisis, the better the chances are of saving the marriage.

Sure enough, Jordan exploded again. But Nathalie stood her ground. She was a wonderful woman, and he did not want to lose her. Suddenly he was highly motivated to get help. About three weeks later, Jordan came back to my office and agreed to get the scan. A couple of weeks went by, and they came back in together. I carefully went over the SPECT results with them, pointing out a slight injury in the right temporal lobe, often causing mood instability, as well as overactivity in the cingulate gyrus.

As a kid, Jordan had been in a motorcycle accident. I had suspected he had suffered some sort of early brain trauma even before I saw the scan. In fact, he was hit so hard on the side of his head that the trauma not only injured his right temporal lobe, but it also collided with the bony part of his forehead, affecting his prefrontal cortex. His "control center" was often off-line, so he had less natural ability to evaluate and censor his words. If you've been married for more than, say, fifteen minutes, you've probably learned that not everything that comes into your mind needs to be said aloud. But I could see from his scan that under stress he lost normal impulse control.

As Jordan watched me explain what his scan meant, all of a sudden he broke down in tears. "I've really been this jerk all these years, haven't I?" he managed to say. I smiled and said, "Yeah, man. You have been."

He smiled back weakly, and I was quick to reassure him. "However, there's something else that is equally as true. There's lots of anti-jerk help for you, available right now. The great news is that if you stick with Dr. Amen's prescribed protocol and continue therapy with me, you may not only save your marriage, but your children may begin to experience their dad as a new man. And when they see you, over time, as a changed human being, they will want a relationship with you. You still have a chance to mend and repair those ties and to be a wonderful grandpa someday."

Over the next few months he stuck with his medical protocol. His marriage grew happier, but his fear was the medication might take the edge off his sales numbers. He need not have worried. His sales went up! He was already the top producer. In fact, his business climbed to a record-level high. To his surprise, he discovered that being kind and flexible was good for business. What do you know?

And yes, if you are wondering, his children, now adults, got interested in what was happening to their formerly volatile father. Eventually, they agreed to come in for a few sessions with him, where repentance, forgiveness, and understanding flowed. (These are the days I *love* being a therapist.) But I have to say this: If this man had had therapy *alone,* I would have never witnessed the amazing progress, the beautiful family reunion. He might have changed for a short bit of time, promising everyone he would be different and better, but sadly, end up breaking all his promises and repeating the obsessive and controlling behaviors.

I've given two examples of men with overactive cingulates thus far. But all's fair in love and brain chemistry. Women also have cingulate issues. Dr. Amen tells the following story about a woman who could not stop herself from obsessive thoughts of cleanliness:

On the outside, Gail was normal. She went to work every day, she was married to her high school sweetheart, and she had two small children. On the inside, Gail felt like a mess. Her husband was ready to leave her, and her children were often withdrawn and upset. Gail was distant from her family and locked into the private hell of obsessive-compulsive disorder. She cleaned her house for hours every night after work. She screamed at her husband and children when anything was out of place. She would become especially hysterical if she saw a piece of hair on the floor, and she was often at the sink washing her hands. She also made her husband and children wash their hands more than ten times a day. She stopped making love to her husband because she couldn't stand the feeling of being messy. On the verge of divorce, Gail and her husband came to see me. At first, her husband was very skeptical about the biological nature of her illness. Gail's brain SPECT study showed marked increased activity in the cingulate system, demonstrating that she really did have trouble shifting her attention.

With this information, I placed Gail on Zoloft. Within six weeks, she had significantly relaxed, her ritualistic behavior had diminished, and she stopped making her kids wash their hands every time they turned around. Her husband couldn't believe the change. Gail was more like the woman he married.[1]

If this chapter rings any familiar bells in your head that remind you of yourself or your mate, if one of you is repeating an unwanted behavior over and over again—a behavior that you know needs to change—it could very well have its root in a brain chemistry problem. What I love about integrating SPECT scans into therapy is that it eliminates the guesswork. We can see, in living color, what is happening deep inside your brain that is holding you back from the happiness you seek but that always eludes you.

To a lesser degree, we all have our "cingulate moments" when we get stuck on a thought (when someone makes a hateful comment, for example, and you can't get it out of your mind) or when you get obsessed with your e-mail or BlackBerry or a video game. So even if you or your mate doesn't have raging cingulate issues, the following tips can help if either of you ever gets in "stuck mode" under stress or becomes increasingly focused on a new activity—and you both know you need a break from a potential addiction . . . especially if it is draining energy from your marriage.

TEN TIPS TO HELP CALM THE OVERFOCUSED BRAIN

1. Eat some carbs.

When someone has a "stuck cingulate," often under stress, what the brain needs is serotonin (the relaxing feel-good neurotransmitter) and not so much dopamine (the energizing neurotransmitter). In mild cases of obsession with a negative thought, you can help yourself to let go of the "bone" with a shift in what you are eating.

The calming effect of serotonin can often be felt in thirty minutes or less by eating foods high in natural sugars or carbohydrates. A banana or cereal with milk is just one good example. Best choices are fruits or breads and cereals with plenty of fiber so that the natural sugars don't enter the bloodstream too quickly. Fiber helps slow down the process, leaving you calmer without the sugar "shakes." Cerebral serotonin levels can also be raised by eating foods rich in tryptophan, such as chicken, turkey, salmon, beef, peanut butter, eggs, green peas, potatoes, and milk.

Many people unknowingly trigger cognitive inflexibility (the psychological term for a stuck cingulate) by eating diets that are low in L-tryptophan. For example, high-protein, low-carbohydrate diets recommended for low dopamine states (related to prefrontal cortex underactivity) often make cingulate problems worse.

If you are feeling overfocused and unable to wind down, try having a whole wheat- or high fiber-pasta–based dinner. Or maybe try a mashed potato or rice bowl with bits of meat and veggies thrown in. A small bowl of cereal or yogurt or cream of wheat makes a great winding-down bedtime snack.

2. Take supplements.

Low serotonin levels and increased cingulate activity are often associated with worrying, moodiness, emotional rigidity, and irritability. St. John's wort, L-tryptophan, and 5-HTP are helpful for cingulate gyrus overactivity. (Note: don't use any two or more of these supplements together at one time. Choose one, and see how it does alone first. This is a good rule of thumb for adding any supplements to your diet. Take one at a time, starting with the lowest dosage.)

St. John's wort seems to be best at increasing serotonin availability in the brain. Dr. Amen usually suggests a starting dosage of St. John's wort at 300 mg a day for children, 300 mg twice a day for teens, and 600 mg in the morning and 300 mg at night for adults. He sometimes encourages adults to talk to their doctor about going as high as 1800 mg. The bottle should say that it contains 0.3 percent hypericin, which is believed to be the active ingredient of St. John's wort.

I have seen SPECT studies done before and after showing that St. John's wort has helped to decrease cingulate gyrus overactivity. It clearly decreases cingulate gyrus hyperactivity for many patients. It also helps with moodiness and trouble shifting attention. Unfortunately, I have also seen it decrease prefrontal cortex activity, turning the overfocused lover into a slightly scattered lover. One of the women in the study said, "I'm happier, but I'm dingier." When cingulate symptoms are present with ADD symptoms (such as feeling "dingier"), it's important to use St. John's wort with a stimulating substance like L-tyrosine or a stimulant such as Adderall. It has been reported that St. John's wort increases sun sensitivity, which means you could get sunburned more easily and therefore need to be careful outdoors. An important note: You do not want to take a stimulating supplement like L-tyrosine or a medication like Adderall without first stabilizing the temporal lobes, if temporal lobe symptoms are present. Avoid any energy pills of any kind even if they claim to be all-natural and safe. There is a specific order we use in calming the brain. If you suspect you may have temporal lobe issues as discussed in the Angry Lover chapter, then don't use stimulating medications or supplements, and avoid foods such as caffeine or too much protein, which can also cause flashes of anger.

There have also been some recent studies with inositol, from the B vitamin family, which you can get from a health-food store. In doses of 12 to 20 milligrams a day, it has been shown to decrease moodiness, depression, and overfocus issues.

Do not take St. John's wort, L-tryptophan, or 5-HTP with prescribed antidepressants unless under the close supervision, and at the recommendation, of your physician. In fact, whether you choose to use medication or supplements, it is imperative that you do so under the advice of a doctor, and preferably one familiar with brain systems.

Finally, many people with stuck thoughts find that using GABA or a combination of GABA with other relaxing ingredients may help them relax, especially when thoughts are going around and around in the evening before bed. (Of these, I prefer Stress-Relax Pharma GABA by Natural Factors.) Amino acids are one of the best supplements to use with the fewest side effects and can usually be taken on an empty stomach. Some books I recommend that will give very specific details on how to use aminos to help balance your mood are *The Mood Cure* by Julia Ross, *Natural Highs* by Hyla Cass and Patrick Holford, and my previous book, *This Is Your Brain on Joy*. One of the benefits of an amino acid such as GABA is that it works very quickly, but it only stays in your system for a few hours. This is why it works very well in helping calm you enough for sleep or in a highly stressful moment. However, you generally have to take supplements more often than medication.

As we age, melatonin also decreases, and many people find that taking melatonin at night helps them relax and get the rest they need.

3. Find the right medications.

Once again, it is important to note that a person with an overactive cingulate is often made worse by the stimulant medications, especially if the cingulate is not first calmed by a serotonin-boosting protocol. The gerbil wheel from hell can go into hyper-speed when using such stimulant medications as Ritalin, Adderall, Focalin, Vyvanse, and Concerta. The problem is not inattention, as with ADD, but overattention. When you give these people a stimulant medication, they tend to focus more on the thoughts they get stuck on. The best medications for this problem tend to be the anti-obsessive antidepressants, which increase the neurotransmitter serotonin in the brain. I have nicknamed these medications "anti-stuck medications." At the time of this writing there are ten medications that are commonly used to increase serotonin in the brain. These medications include Effexor (venlafaxine), Prozac (fluoxetine), Paxil (paroxetine), Zoloft (sertraline), Anafranil (clomipramine), Desyrel (trazodone), Celexa (citalopram), Remeron (mirtazapine), and Luvox (fluvoxamine).

4. Try soothing self-talk.

When you catch yourself starting to tense up and get overfocused, use a couple of phrases to remind yourself to relax and let go. Take a few seconds to breathe slowly and say calming phrases to yourself, such as:

- "Chill, buddy."
- "It's not worth the upset. Let it go."
- "He may be having a bad day. Cut him some slack here. You aren't perfect, either."
- "No big deal. No worries."
- "Re-la-ax. Breathe. Let it go."

Or memorize a soothing go-to verse, such as John 14:27: "I am leaving you with a gift—peace of mind and heart. And the peace I give is a gift the world cannot give. So don't be troubled or afraid" (NLT).

An excellent book full of relaxing self-talk is by life coach and recovering perfectionist Joan Webb, titled *The Relief of Imperfection*.

5. Tap away the looping thought.

There is a self-help technique that is growing in popularity because of the ease in using it and because it works wonders with many people. You can get a free lesson in using what has been termed the Emotional Freedom Technique, or EFT, from the Web site www.emofree.com. I have used it with great success with clients and taught them to use it on themselves when they get swept away by agitation, though I do realize that it is a bit controversial. The brain science behind tapping or eye-movement (EMDR) therapy is that it is a physical activity that breaks up a looping thought, and helps you shift gears to a better, loftier, happier state of mind. It doesn't cost anything but your time and willingness to try it, and if it doesn't work for you, you are not out any monetary investment.

6. Walk before you talk, preferably with music.

Physical exercise of any kind will also help you disengage from a compulsive thought or agitated frame of mind. Before you start the blame game or unload your frustration on your mate, say, "Honey, I need to walk for a few minutes before we talk. It's for the good of our marriage!" Then take off. Better yet, combine walking with an iPod loaded with music to calm the stuck gerbil within. What kind of music? Whatever soothes your soul and puts you in a happy, relaxed frame of mind. For you, it may be Bach; for me, it may be rock 'n' roll oldies; for someone else, it could be praise music or jazz. There are multiple reasons why each of our brains relaxes with certain sounds. Purchasing or creating a "serenity" CD or downloads for your iPod can transport you from Stuckville to Chillville.

7. Collect gratitude instead of grudges.

One of the hardest things for a cingulate-minded person to do is to let go and forgive others of past offenses. In truth, deep down, people with stuck cingulates are even harder on themselves. But here's the rub. The kind of guilt an overfocused lover experiences feels more like *shame*—and shame is an emotion that is just too painful for most humans to carry for long. So we will find a way to get rid of the feeling of shame, often by quickly shifting blame or rationalizing wrongdoing, rather than dealing with normal guilt in healthy ways—such as apologies, amends, or asking for God's grace.

I have found that the best way to forgive your spouse in a typical marital spat is to refocus on the good that person has brought to your life. Brain research shows us that we cannot be angry and grateful at the same time. One emotion knocks out the other, neurologically speaking. So, think of five to ten positive things your spouse brings to your life. Do this gratitude exercise *before* you even try to forgive your mate of a wrongdoing. Just let the good he or she brings to your life float to the surface of your mind. Better yet, write it down.

Now, remember a time when you've failed, messed up, or been thoughtless, and needed forgiveness. Who in your life gave you grace when you needed it most? Feel the gratitude and freedom that you felt when someone (Was it Jesus? Your husband or wife? A friend? A parent?) forgave you and gave you a clean slate.

As you are remembering the good things about your mate and your own need for grace, ask the Lord to take away your need for vengeance and anger toward your spouse and to replace your grudge with gratitude, praying for God's mercy to all of us flawed and failing humans.

Repeat as often as necessary! Forgiveness will soon flow more easily as gratitude takes the place of grudges.

One disclaimer: *This forgiveness exercise is not meant as a way to throw pink paint over truly painful or recurring issues of hurt that need to be addressed in a marriage, or deep wounds from a spouse that are more serious in nature. When trust has been damaged or destroyed, the issue is deeper. Forgiveness takes longer, and restoration of trust even longer. Abuse, adultery, abandonment, and addiction are the four As that will require special help to forgive, a wise, benevolent counselor at your side to help you navigate these particularly rough seas. This forgiveness exercise works best for typical, minor marital spats or irritations.*

8. *Breathe deeply, and open your focus.*

It's amazing how often we forget to breathe deeply, especially when we are stuck in overdrive. Take a few minutes to walk outside and get some fresh oxygen in your lungs and your brain. Look up at the sky, soak in some sun, look at the horizon. Broaden your visual focus, acknowledge the periphery, and take in the bigger picture of the world. This simple visual exercise has been shown to relax the heart rate and give perspective on our lives. When we get tense, even our eyes get singly focused and overfocused. For more information on this, you might enjoy reading the book *The Open-Focus Brain* by Les Fehmi and Jim Robbins.

9. *Act as if you are an islander.*

If you have ever played "let's pretend," then you know how taking on the role of another character can make you feel the emotions of the part you are playing. Those from Polynesian cultures often look at the West and shake their heads at our high stress levels. *What's their hurry?* they wonder at us. One way to slow down on the inside is to imagine you are in Hawaii or Tahiti. Pretend you are a native islander. For just a few minutes think, *Don't worry; be happy!* Put your imaginary bare feet in the warm sand; feel the ocean breeze; listen to a ukulele. Take a mental vacation to an island, *mahn!* Then come back to reality a little more laid-back and refreshed, and less hurried.

A wonderful book about the "oceanic mind-set" is called *The Pleasure Prescription* by the late Dr. Paul Pearsall. And a follow-up book called *Partners in Pleasure* is equally fascinating. Dr. Pearsall was a longtime resident of Hawaii and gloriously married to one woman for many decades. There are some lessons about relaxation and calm from our island neighbors that we Americans could definitely stand to learn. The books are now out of print, but you can find them for a song through Amazon's used book sellers. Aloha!

10. *Daily, resign your control of the universe to the true Creator.*

I remember hearing on a talk show how down-home info-tainer, country-western star, and self-confessed former controlling human being Naomi Judd said that every morning she resigns control of the universe to God. It's one way of humorously reminding herself how small she really is and Who is really in charge. (In fact, she wrote a chapter called "Resign as General Manager of the Universe" in the book *The Transparent Life*.)

A great prayer to start your morning might be, "Dear God, I resign control of the universe to You again. I'll get in the backseat now, and let You do the driving today."

TEN TIPS TO HELP YOUR OVERFOCUSED MATE

1. Remember that his or her crisis doesn't have to be your emergency.

When the one you love is having a bad-mood day, you might be tempted to wonder what you did to cause this reaction or mood. When your partner is stressed-out, stop and go to another area of the house, if needed, to give yourself a little distance from the crisis. Most likely it really isn't about you, and you don't have to take on his or her blue day or temporary tantrum. Don't automatically assume responsibility for how your mate is feeling, even though you love her deeply. It really won't help if both of you get agitated.

Sometimes giving your mate the gift of space is truly the most loving thing you can do for both of you.

2. Support, don't fix.

Clearly and honestly look to see if you have any true role in this upset. Calmly ask, "Is there something I can do differently to help ease your stress?" Another great question is, "How can I best support you right now?" If you can help and are asked nicely, by all means, do what you can to aid and comfort your sweetheart. However, it is never okay to be anyone's "punching bag," literally or figuratively.

Two great resources are *Boundaries in Marriage* by Henry Cloud and John Townsend and *I Don't Have to Make Everything All Better* by Gary B. Lundberg and Joy Saunders Lundberg, two classics that will help you protect your heart when your mate is beginning to use unhealthy controlling behaviors.

3. Create your own happy hour.

If your mate is uptight, having trouble disconnecting from the day, and you want to bring calm so you both can connect, help create an environment that soothes. For example, you can use calming scents that you know he loves. Men tend to like cinnamon and vanilla (reminds them of Mom's home cooking). Women often like baby powder or lavender to relax by. You can light scented candles or pour some scented oil or bubble bath into a tub. Epsom salt in a tub also adds magnesium through the skin, which relaxes both the mind and achy muscles. Be sure to ask what scents he or she enjoys because some scents could bring about *more* irritation. Just ask . . . or notice.

Serve a higher-carb meal, like spaghetti, or a milk-and-fruit smoothie for dessert.

Turn on some relaxing music.

Invite him to go on a walk or exchange back rubs.

Pay attention to the transitional times during the daily routines—waking up and getting to work, coming home from work, and going to bed. Do what you can to create little rituals that help your mate let go of one activity and prepare for the next. Transitions are typically hard for overfocused lovers. You may be able to help ease them in and out of one activity to the next.

4. Open the cage door.

When overfocused lovers get stuck on a "my way or the highway" train of thought, step aside and say something like, "Whatever you think. You've got a good mind, and I know you'll do the right thing and figure out the best plan." Don't get caught in a never-ending debate. It's an alligator roll you most often can't win. Just open the cage door, and let them fly in any direction they choose. Often they'll fly right back into your court and be willing to listen to your reasoning.

I will confess right now that it is a challenge to be married to an overfocused lover who leans toward being a controlling lover. But I have been astounded at the creativity of husbands and wives who have learned how to handle their partners' overfocused, inflexible moods like relational geniuses. Gus Portokalos, the father from the movie *My Big Fat Greek Wedding*, is a classic study in old-fashioned control. His wife, Maria, had obviously spent decades learning how to handle her husband's moods . . . as masterfully as any trained psychologist.

5. Use reverse psychology.

Often cingulate people automatically say no without really thinking. One way to shake them off of their prescribed answer is to ask questions differently. Rather than say, "I want to go to the movies tonight," you may have better luck saying, "I was thinking about going to see that action-thriller tonight. You don't want to go, do you?" Or "I am sure you don't want to go on a walk with me, right?" Often a controlling person will answer, "Why wouldn't I want to go on a walk with you? Of *course* I'd love to go on a walk with you." They do it for the sheer joy of contradicting you. (I've started calling this "pulling a Maria Portokalos.")

6. Be compassionate about his or her need for minimal order.

Although there is no way that people can live in a perfectly ordered home all the time, acknowledge that your mate will probably be more stressed when the environment is a mess. Talk about a compromise. Betsy says, "My husband loves order and, of course, I am a messy who likes little nests all over the house. I love him, and I see how much more relaxed he is when we keep the living room and kitchen picked up and fairly clean most of the time. I have my own messy spaces, and he doesn't ask that I keep a perfect home, but he so appreciates the effort I expend to keep the main living areas neat. And he helps out, so I love to give him this little gift of order as often as I can in a few designated spaces."

7. Understand the compulsions, but know when to seek help.

"When my wife gets stressed," says one man, "she likes to organize the kitchen. Yes, spices not only go in alphabetical order but they have a little Spice Island Kingdom of their own. Seeing her cabinets in order just gives her such a happy hit of calm. I figure there are worse ways to let off steam!"

One husband goes to his stamp collection when feeling out of control. His wife is compassionate. "When his parents divorced, George was just eleven years old. He could lose himself in the world of organizing stamps or collecting magazines. It was a micro world that he could control when his family life was falling apart. Now, when I see him reach for a puzzle to put together or stamps to order, I think of that little boy who just needed to control *something* in his chaotic world. And I smile, make us some cocoa, pull up my chair, and help him work the puzzle or find the stamps. It means a lot to him that I understand the serenity he gets from these little hobbies. We've found that a compassionate approach helps turn potential irritants into endearments."

Know that when your mate is under stress, compulsions to bring order will be greater. And that is okay; most of us can roll with those times. However, if the compulsion gets out of hand and your mate literally cannot stop organizing or hand washing or ordering others around—it is time to seek some professional help. I urge you to see someone who is very familiar with brain imaging so that if medication is needed, you can be sure it is the exact, right protocol to help the one you love best.

8. Be a noticer.

Think like a research scientist and note the times when your mate is most relaxed. What is he doing? What is she listening to? What did he eat? Did she exercise? Who was he with? Note any patterns to his level of calm, and share what you've noticed with him. Talk about ways to help increase the general level of tranquillity in your home, your lives, and your relationship.

9. Be aware of hormonal issues.

Women with severe PMS will often show overactive cingulates just before and during their menstrual cycles. But a few days later in their cycles, their scans may look perfectly normal. Hormones create the neurotransmitters that affect our moods. If you notice a cyclical pattern to controlling or agitated behaviors, consider suggesting she have her hormones checked. Some women need a little medication or supplementation for just part of the month.

One woman said, "Normally, I am the most laid-back, messy person on the planet. But just before my period, I turn into Super-Clean Nazi. A stray sock on the floor that I might not have even noticed two days earlier seems suddenly a personal affront! I am just so agitated with everyone, and my desire for order soars off the charts. It is during these times that I really empathize with those struggling with OCD issues. I feel temporarily kidnapped by an obsessive controlling personality." Husbands can help by charting their wives' cycles, on their own personal calendars, and doing everything they can to help minimize stress and simply "be there" in whatever way their wives need support during those few difficult hormonal days.

Men, too, can have hormonal issues—often too much testosterone that causes their cingulates, to flame like crazy. Thankfully, more and more doctors are recognizing the connection between hormones and neurotransmitters and everyone's happiness. Using your computer search engine, enter "bioidentical hormones," then "MD" (or the kind of doctor you prefer), and finally the name of your city. A list of doctors who are well versed in bioidentical hormones should pop up. Then research from there the ones with the best experience, highest recommendations, and/or who are covered by your insurance. (More information on women and hormones can be found in the appendices.)

I must tell you that the research on hormones and the brain is getting more fascinating as the months roll by. I feel we are just on the cutting edge of some breakthroughs in balancing hormones as a way to help balance brain health.

10. Pay attention to blood sugar.

Many people are very sensitive to drops in their blood sugar and will get suddenly cranky and out of sorts when they've not eaten anything in too long a period of time. Note if this is possibly true about your spouse. See if his or her need for rest, food, or liquid plays into any sudden need for control or easily agitated state of mind. "My husband would completely change personalities when he got hungry and his blood sugar dove. I began carrying little packets of nuts or a fiber bar everywhere we went to help keep his blood sugar steady on trips or when we'd be away from the house, watching the kids play soccer. It's not only compassion for him, but it's being kind to myself. I like him to be in a good mood, and this little preventive helps so much. He also gets this way when he needs a nap or a good night's sleep. Sometimes even my four-year-old will say, 'Daddy needs a naptime!'"

Even if you are not a generally obsessive or controlling person, everyone experiences times when they feel as though their "cingulate gyrus is on fire." Use these hints whenever you or your mate is feeling stressed, obsessed, or mentally caught in a negative loop. We've all been there at one time or another.

Please rate yourself on each of the symptoms listed below, using the following scale:

0=Never 1=Rarely 2=Occasionally 3=Frequently 4=Very Frequently
N/A=Not Applicable/Not Known
   (You answer in one column, your mate in the other column.)

____ ____ 1. Frequent feelings of sadness
____ ____ 2. Moodiness
____ ____ 3. Negativity
____ ____ 4. Low energy
____ ____ 5. Irritability
____ ____ 6. Decreased interest in others
____ ____ 7. Decreased interest in things that are usually fun or
         pleasurable
____ ____ 8. Feelings of hopelessness about the future
____ ____ 9. Feelings of helplessness or powerlessness
____ ____ 10. Feeling dissatisfied or bored
____ ____ 11. Excessive guilt
____ ____ 12. Suicidal feelings
____ ____ 13. Crying spells
____ ____ 14. Lowered interest in things usually considered fun
____ ____ 15. Sleep changes (too much or too little)
____ ____ 16. Appetite changes (too much or too little)
____ ____ 17. Chronic low self-esteem

Results: If five or more of your answers are rated 3 or 4, you may need to consider an antidepressant or a supplement with antidepressant qualities.

From Amen Brain Subsystem Checklist, used by permission from Dr. Daniel Amen and the Amen Clinic.

CHAPTER SIX

The Blue Mood Lover
(Deep Limbic System)

He ate, worked, loved, dreamed and played in this garment of heaviness, weighed down as if he were wearing a leaden bathrobe—trudging daily through the murky despondency that sucked the color out of everything.

—WILLIAM P. YOUNG, *THE SHACK*
(DESCRIPTION OF THE GREAT SADNESS)

Depression is toxic to marriage. As it turns out, when either Mama *or Papa* ain't happy, ain't nobody happy in their marriage. Being married to someone who struggles with blue moods takes its toll on both partners.

"There is a growing body of research indicating that mental health and unhappy marriages are closely entwined," writes lead researcher Mark A. Whisman, PhD, with the University of Colorado at Boulder.[1] In this particular study, Whisman and his colleagues recruited 774 married couples from seven states. Each partner was tested for depression, anxiety, and whether he felt he had a happy or unhappy marriage. They found (not surprisingly, in my opinion) that when one partner tended toward depression, the other spouse began to struggle with being happy as well, especially with being happy with the state of their marriage.

The researchers also tested for anxiety, but it was in marriages where depression was the third silent "partner" that couples felt the most unhappy in their marriages. Having an anxious or fearful spouse tended not to be as dampening to a relationship as having a depressed partner. Of course, this makes sense. When your mate is fearful (we'll talk about that in the next chapter), you may be able to offer soothing comfort. Perhaps you may even feel needed and appreciated.

When someone is feeling depressed, however, everything in his world is colored in shades of gray with outlines of sorrow or heaviness or disappointment. Including the way he views *you*. Needless to say, when your partner is always looking at you through gray-colored glasses, you aren't going to feel terribly positive about him either. There's an old saying that "We fall in love, not so much because of the way we feel about *them,* but how they make us feel about *ourselves* when we are with them." When you are living with a spouse stuck in a blue funk, he doesn't tend to make you feel very good about yourself in his presence. In fact, many partners of depressed spouses long to escape the dark cloud that engulfs them when they are with their low-mood mates.

ESCAPING THE BLACK CLOUD

A friend of mine, Francesca, said, "I remember being on vacation with my first husband, a classic low-mood person all his life. Even as a teenager he was a 'lost puppy dog,' and I, ever the Pollyanna cheerleader, had planned to rescue him and make him happy. I spent nearly thirty years trying to cheer him up before I ran out of happy juice to give him.

"I had hoped and prayed that going on a vacation to gorgeous Victoria, Canada, with its beautiful scenery, and staying in a luxury hotel would perk up my husband's ever-flagging spirits. But, to my sinking heart, I soon realized that he had packed the black cloud and brought it with us. As soon as we got to the hotel room, he fell asleep. I was actually relieved, because while he was asleep, I could slip outside in the sunshine and breathe the fresh air, enjoy the day, walk to a coffee shop, browse a bookstore and—all of this unbridled joy—without a wet blanket dragging behind me.

"It would be a few more years before we divorced and I would get married to a man who 'made his *own* sunshine'—but I remember the ironic, but enormous relief of literally closing the door on the melancholy in that dim hotel room and walking away from my depressed husband into the beautiful daylight. I felt like a bird free from her cage and realized somewhere in my gut that I could not live with the black hole of dreariness that my husband epitomized, for the rest of my life.

"Here's the tragedy: over the decades of our marriage, he'd been to at least three counselors who all told him he should be treated for depression. But he was a proud man, a stubborn redneck-type who refused any sort of professional or medical help. So he kept his pride and lost his wife and family. I know that had he been willing to get help for his chemical imbalance, we probably would be married today. But after three decades of living with a human black cloud, using all the emotional energy I could muster to fight for snippets of joy outside of our marriage, I feared for my own mental health."[2]

Add to the heavy weight that depressed moods already bring to a marriage, the fact that when the limbic system is overactive, the sex drive is often close to defunct, and you've got a formula for a marriage heading into a brick wall.

A PEEK UNDER THE DEEP LIMBIC HOOD

When the limbic system is working well, you are experiencing:

- Feelings of hope, even during difficult times
- Restorative sleep
- Strong self-esteem
- Enjoyment of pleasurable, fun activities where you feel like laughing at a joke or smiling at the simplest experience
- Desire to be with people
- Enjoyment of hugs and being close
- Optimism

When the limbic system is not working well, usually overactive, then the following symptoms may occur:

- Difficulty being grateful for all of the good that God has done in your life
- Irritation at things that usually do not bother you
- Desire to be alone or to socially isolate
- Experiences that used to be fun are no longer of interest (they seem to take too much effort)
- Difficulty going to sleep or staying asleep

- Waking up in the morning and needing everything you've got to just move out of bed
- A lack of motivation to do self-care
- Frequent feelings of hopelessness, helplessness, or excessive guilt. No matter how much you pray, or remind yourself of various scriptural truths, you still feel guilty.
- Extreme mood changes during PMS
- Low energy
- Lack of sexual interest to the extent that it's rare to have a sexual thought
- Loss of appetite
- Weight loss or weight gain

WHY SHE JUMPED

There are many reasons why people sink into depressed moods, and there are many levels of depression, from blue days to chronic low moods to a severe clinical depression. Some depressions are grief-induced or seasonal or cyclical (as in PMS) in nature. Others seem to have a genetic component, the way alcoholism or addictions run in some families. Still others are due to hormonal imbalances or thyroid issues or adrenal burnout.

On occasion there are even multiple reasons for depression that pile up, one on top of another, and create the perfect storm of pain so terrible that some hurting people, so desperate to end their inner suffering, try to end their own precious lives.

Such was the case of Tina Zahn, whose partial story unfolded for the world to see in a nationwide news story of a dramatic police tape. Eventually Tina would write about her journey through depression, attempted suicide, and recovery, in a book called *Why I Jumped,* and tell it to an audience on *Oprah* in the fall of 2007.

Why would a woman who loved God, had a good husband, precious kids, great Christian friends, and was involved in a loving church, drive her car to a Green Bay bridge, some 200 feet above the water below, get out of her car, and jump off?

Police, alerted by her husband, who feared she might harm herself, followed in hot pursuit. With his car-cam rolling, one brave officer followed his instincts instead of the rules. While risking going over the edge himself, he reached over the ledge at the last possible second and caught Tina by her wrist, *after she had completely disappeared from sight*—a split-second decision that could only be called miraculous.

In the introduction to *Why I Jumped*, Tina shares, "This is a book that if you're not prepared for it, could wear you out with drama. Many women who suffer from post-partum depression get over it quickly. They had a good childhood, no other psychological issues, and the chemical imbalance soon returns to normal. End of story. But if there are other emotional traumas in a woman's life that haven't been dealt with, the Post-Partum trigger can drop a huge emotional hydrogen bomb in a woman's life.

"I'm the first to admit that my story has some extreme elements to it. I didn't just have PPD. I had PPD and repressed memories of actual and long-term sexual abuse by someone I trusted. I didn't just have PPD and sexual abuse; my mother also rejected me when she discovered the abuse. I didn't just have the PPD, the sexual abuse, and the rejection; but the residual effects of those things led to my making bad decisions, which in turn produced other hurtful events. It was a never ending cycle that led me to the bridge that morning."[3]

Though Tina had endured a lifetime packaged with pain, after God gave her a second chance at life, she found the help she needed to smile again. Through "the gift of friendship, a strong measure of faith, a loving spouse, and some good medications," Tina writes, "I have progressed from wanting to end it all to having much more to look forward to than I could have ever imagined."[4]

Tina had been on many antidepressants in her past, but none had worked until her doctor happened upon a prescription that finally did the job and blew away the dark clouds in her brain. But in reading about Tina's story, I could see that the doctors had used the trial-and-error approach. I could not help but think, *If Tina had received a brain scan, we could have helped pinpoint her exact med needs and possibly have saved her decades of inner torment.* Oh, the years that are wasted and lost because of an overactive, undiagnosed, or misdiagnosed limbic system. Not to mention the marriages dissolved and worse, lives lost.

GRIEF OR DEPRESSION: A SIDE-BY-SIDE COMPARISON

Characteristics of Grief	Characteristics of Depression
A normal, complicated response to loss that causes distress	Generalized distress—loss of interest, pleasure
May experience some physical symptoms of distress	Somatic distress, hopelessness, guilt
Still able to look toward the future	No sense of positive future
Passive wish for death	Suicidal ideation not uncommon
Retains capacity for pleasure	Bored, lack of interest and expression
Still able to express feelings and humor	Persistent blank or expressionless look on the face, negative self-image
Comes in waves	Constant, unremitting
Can cope with distress on own or with supportive listening	Change in capacity to enjoy life or things that were formerly pleasurable
Pharmacotherapy for grief is an exception, not the rule	Often requires intervention with medication, therapy
	May require combined psychosocial interventions and pharmacotherapy
	Advanced disease and pain

HORMONAL DEPRESSION IN WOMEN

Because PMS, PPD, and menopause can cause special kinds of depression, I've decided to devote a special appendix to these issues (Appendix D). I hope it is helpful. Hormonal fluctuations can really take a toll on women and the men who love them.

NORMAL GRIEF OR A CLINICAL DEPRESSION?

After a tragedy or deep loss, grief mimics depression. When clients come to see me after the death of a loved one or a divorce, they often wonder if they are just moving through grief, or are clinically depressed, or both. Here's some of what I share to help us figure that out together. Sometimes a deep loss can trigger someone who is genetically predisposed to depression into a major clinical depression. So I never say, "You are just in grief, and all these feelings are normal" until I've done a lot more information gathering.

Definition of a Clinical Depression

A depressive disorder is a syndrome (group of symptoms) that reflects a sad mood exceeding normal sadness or grief. More specifically, the sadness of depression is characterized by a greater intensity, duration, and more severe symptoms and functional disabilities than is normal. Depression symptoms are characterized not only by negative thoughts, moods, and behaviors, but also by specific changes in bodily functions (for example, irregular eating, sleeping, crying spells, and decreased libido). At this point the entire nervous system in the brain has changed so much that it causes physical conditions, including physical pain.

WHAT DEPRESSION LOOKS LIKE

Below is a scan of a brain in pain, showing too much activity in the deep limbic area.

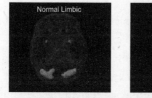

Normal and depressed brain, side-by-side comparison

THE DEPRESSION DETECTIVE AT WORK

John was one of those men who had been slowly sabotaging his marriage because of wrongly treated depression. By the time the two of them came into my office, John's wife, Judy, had given up on any possibility of their marriage changing. "John's not interested in doing anything, ever. He won't go to a movie or play tennis—something we used to love doing together—or even take an evening walk. I cannot remember when he reached for me with any desire to make love at all. He used to initiate lovemaking regularly, and I would always respond with enthusiasm. So it's not like I've rejected him and made him fearful of reaching out to me—in fact, quite the opposite!"

Judy wiped at her eyes. "I feel so undesired and unattractive. My body craves loving touch. But even after our general practitioner gave him an antidepressant, John doesn't want me. I have given up trying to interest him in sex anymore."

As I took down their history, I noted that John's loss of desire seemed to coincide with a recent career disappointment. John had come to believe that he would never get the management position he'd wanted in his company. His career, he felt, had capped, and this was "as good as it was ever going to get." The loss of his dream to climb a little higher on the corporate ladder left him despondent. Now that he was in his fifties and would experience periodic erectile dysfunction (normal for men at this age), he lacked the motivation to figure out what was happening to his libido. So he'd just given up. In fact, his lack of sexual prowess only seemed to confirm what he'd experienced at work. *I've lost my potency as a man,* he thought.

John explained, "I just keep on keeping on. I never miss a day of work. I get the job done. In these economic times I should just be grateful I have a job. Right?"

"Well, we'll get to that issue," I said, "but first, tell me if anything else that you once enjoyed has gone . . . flat."

"I used to love our church, and enjoyed serving there, helping out the youth group. Being around those young kids used to energize me; now I just seem to draw comparisons. They are young and virile, and I feel like an old has-been."

Judy sighed. "Can you help us, Dr. Henslin? I feel myself going numb toward this man I used to feel so passionate about. More and more I want to escape from the dark cloud and find some joy, anywhere out there. I'm in a vulnerable place and I know it."

John was sincerely caught in a brain fog so thick he couldn't even see how bad it had gotten. He didn't think he was that miserable to live with, assuming he'd bottled up and hidden most of his inner anguish. He hadn't realized what his moods were doing to his wife and also to his teenage children, who were avoiding him more and more. The lens of depression changes us slowly and subtly so that a person doesn't even realize that the colorful, high-definition life he once enjoyed, in full surround-sound, has gradually diminished to a life that resembles a fuzzy picture on an old 1950s black-and-white television. You still get a picture, you hear it . . . but it is all so fuzzy that you fall asleep before the show is over.

John's scores on the Blue Mood Lover checklist indicated that he had moderate to severe depression. "But Dr. Henslin," he said, "I started taking an antidepressant a few months ago."

"This tells me, John, that this particular medication is obviously not working for you. And not only that, but SSRIs, the family of drugs you are taking, commonly cause sexual side effects. Here's what I'd like you to do. Get a complete physical with blood panels that will test your testosterone levels and screen for diabetes. Also, I'd like you to have a sleep study because lack of sleep, especially deep, high-quality sleep, can also contribute to depression. You may not even be aware that you aren't going into the deep, delta wave sleep that you need to replenish and restart your brain, so to speak. You may have sleep apnea. Untreated sleep apnea will increase your risk of high blood pressure and other cardiovascular problems, and will cause two times the risk of developing dementia or Alzheimer's than the normal population."

In addition, I asked John to do the following:

- Keep a food and exercise diary to determine his level of physical activity and to discern whether or not nutrition was impacting his levels of depression and anxiety.
- Get a SPECT imaging study to determine with more accuracy how to help balance his brain chemistry. A SPECT scan would reveal whether John's low moods were stemming from depression and, more importantly, help us pinpoint what type of low mood he was battling.
- Ask his MD to perform a blood panel to discover his testosterone and thyroid levels and a fasting glucose study (to determine hypoglycemia or possibly type-2 diabetes, both of which can lead to depression along with a myriad of other physical problems).

Judy seemed hopeful that there might be some solutions to underlying problems with her husband's moods, which helped her hold on a little longer.

The results of John's tests told the tale. The brain is sneaky. All the thoughts and feelings we have, that we believe to be so accurate, are colored by any and all of the imbalances in our brains. That means that our feelings about something or someone can be very far from the truth due to neurotransmitters and hormonal, nutritional, emotional, and spiritual issues. John's test results follow, along with my advice to help him take his low mood up a few notches . . . for the sake of his marriage.

Test	Results	Steps to take
SPECT scan	John's SPECT results showed severe overactivity in the thalamo-limbic system (i.e., severe depression), and instability in his temporal lobes (mood swings). The limbic system plays a role in emotionally charged memories, sexual interest, and desire. His lack of sexual interest was stemming from the anti-depressant medication he was on and an ineffective treatment of his depression.	Due to John's sensitivity to the SSRI family of medications, together we decided to try a supplement route. He would go on a combination of high levels of omega-3 fatty acids (fish oil), SAM-e, and 5-HTP. Ginkgo and L-tyrosine would be added to make sure he stayed mentally sharp (dopamine to his prefrontal cortex) while the other supplements calmed anxiety and raised his serotonin naturally.
Testosterone	His testosterone levels were below normal. Low testosterone can cause lack of drive, motivation, and sexual interest. Testosterone levels also influence serotonin in the brain. Muscle tone and muscle mass are also affected.	His primary care MD prescribed a testosterone cream that John applied to the inside of his thigh.
Nutrition	His blood study showed that he was at high risk of developing type-2 diabetes, and also his cholesterol levels were dangerously high.	John gave up fast food. A recent study showed that living close to fast food restaurants increases your risk of stroke! He began eating breakfast at home (a fruit and fiber protein shake) and learned to make a balanced protein, carb, and fat lunch to take to work. He and his wife began walking each night for 45 minutes to one hour to talk and pray together. Omega-3 fatty acids also helped lower cholesterol.

John's turnaround was rather remarkable. As he learned to love and care for his own body and soul—the whole person—John's brain, heart, and mind woke up to life again. In his new, improved, happier, and more focused state, he came up with an innovative product that impressed his boss at work. So much so that when a new position was created in the company—VP of Information Systems—John got the job.

As Judy saw John's happiness rise, she also felt new waves of passion within her for the fun guy she thought was gone forever. She risked reaching toward him and he risked reaching back, and in time, their love life enjoyed a romantic renaissance.

Does this sound unrealistic? Like a fairy tale? I assure you that not only is this story true (while changing names and a couple of circumstances to protect identities), it is one of a hundred just like it. This is why I love my job—especially since I started to understand the importance of every husband and wife bringing their best, most focused, calm, and happy brains to the altar of marriage.

Are you consistently feeling less happy than you want to? Here's a prescription for you to try.

TEN TIPS TO LIFT THE BLUE MOOD LOVER

1. Chop wood; carry water; knit a sweater.

Interestingly, depression is much lower in countries where people use their hands and do physical labor that yields meaningful rewards—such as food to eat, clothes to wear, and wood for the fire to keep warm. It is astounding how, even in third-world countries where the economy is terrible and freedom is often limited, people who get out in their gardens, produce their own food, and generally create the things that help them survive, have a small fraction of the depression that we have in our country. The Amish and others who live an agrarian lifestyle have much lower depression rates, as did, apparently, our grandmothers and grandfathers.

Scientists are finding that our brains are literally wired for meaningful work that involves at least some physical labor, preferably out of doors. But even crafting and homemaking activities such as knitting or cooking seem to calm anxiety and elevate moods. In her book *Lifting Depression*, Dr. Kelly Lambert talks about the discovery of an effort-driven reward loop (EDR) that, when activated, increases our happiness. When the effort involves your hands in the task, it seems to work even better. ("Give your brain a hand!")

2. *Get a boost through nutrition.*

To know what sort of diet is helpful for a particular type of depression, it is important to know what kind of depressive symptoms a person is experiencing. If you are feeling lethargic, then you probably need a diet and perhaps supplements that will help stimulate your brain's production of dopamine, the stimulating neurotransmitter. If your depression is more anxiety-based or is a low mood that is stuck in a negative-thinking loop, then you will probably be most helped by a diet that increases serotonin, the calming neurotransmitter. In *The Mood Cure*, author Julia Ross suggests that low endorphins make people highly sensitive; they don't just cry at sad movies, but at commercials with soft music—even if those commercials are about toilet paper. They feel thin-skinned. Some people need calming foods before bed, and others need energy-producing foods during the day.

For all types of depression, follow the Joy Diet in Appendix A. In addition, it is important to do the following:

- Eat regularly. You are robbing your body of good mood nutrients when you skip a meal, even breakfast.
- Eat three good meals daily, plus healthy snacks. Include some protein in every snack: try peanut butter on a banana; sprinkle almonds or walnuts on yogurt or a small bowl of nutritious cereal; eat apple slices with string cheese. This will keep your blood sugar steady and your energy up.
- Try to get at least 20 grams of protein per meal, but include plenty of fruits and vegetables so your digestive system can handle it well. Here are a few ways to get your 20 or more grams of protein in:

  - 3 eggs
  - 3 oz tuna, 8 oz cottage cheese
  - 1½ c beans

- 3–4 oz (a palm full) of meat; try to have fish (salmon is best) at least two times a week, more if possible.

- If you suspect that you are low in serotonin (need more calming foods in your diet), incorporate more tryptophan-rich protein into your diet. Some of the world's best sources of tryptophan-rich protein are turkey, cheese (cheddar and parmesan), chicken, beef, shrimp, pork, fish, seeds (sesame and sunflower), eggs, milk, yogurt, cottage cheese, chickpeas, and peanuts. In addition to these protein-based sources, other good sources of tryptophan are: chocolate, oats, bananas, mangoes, dried dates, rice, and potatoes.

- A good rule of thumb is that the more energy you need, the more you should stick with mostly fish, meat, cottage cheese, or eggs to get the big protein bang in your food. As the day winds down, you may want to make your last snack be a bowl of cereal with milk and a banana, or some rice pudding, or try warmed yogurt with brown rice and chopped dates. The lactose in milk and the natural sugar in bananas and dates will make you calm and sleepy.

- Eat dark chocolate! To keep sugar low, melt unsweetened dark chocolate in the microwave and mix in the sweetener Stevia to taste, then berries, and chopped almonds or nuts. Let chill or freeze on a plate, and break it up like candy bark. Enjoy a few pieces when you get that chocolate craving.

3. Try supplements.

All of the following recommendations are adapted or taken from *The Mood Cure* by Julia Ross.[5] I highly recommended that you purchase this book and read it for yourself. It's entertaining, readable, and doable. One benefit of trying supplements for low to moderate depressive symptoms is that if they work, many people only have to take them for a few months to restore their body's balance. If you have the time and patience to try amino acid or herbal supplementation—and you aren't in too much emotional pain—it could really be worth your while.

Note: You may have a combination of symptoms, and if so, you may treat them with appropriate supplements for each symptom. For example, you may need energy for your daytime depression, but a calming supplement to help anxiety at night.

- *For all*

    1–3 capsules of fish oil. Fish oil has been a near-miracle supplement for many who suffer from depression, and especially from bipolar disorder and its less intense cousin, cyclothymia.

- *For depression with lethargy*

    Need: Focus and energy

    Recommendation: L-tyrosine (500 mg)

    1–4 capsules up to 3 times a day. Try one capsule before you increase your dose, and cut back if you feel agitated. And/or L-phenylananine (200–500 mg): 1–4 capsules in the morning and midmorning; 1–3 capsules at midafternoon.

    If these do not help enough, you can add or substitute the following and see if they work better with your body:

    SAM-e (400 mg): 2 midmorning and 2 midafternoon

    Grape seed extract (100 mg): 1 at breakfast and 1 at lunch

- *For depression with anxiety*

    Need: Calming

    Recommendation: 5-HTP (50 mg)

    1–3 capsules at midafternoon; 1–3 at bedtime. Start with 50 mg, and if you don't get relief within an hour, increase to 2 capsules. If needed, add a third dose in about another hour. You've established the dose that works for you. If you awaken at night and can't get back to sleep, you may also take 1–2 more capsules. Or tryptophan (500 mg): 1–3 at midafternoon; 1–3 at bedtime. (For a very few people, tryptophan works better than 5-HTP, but the vast majority do better on 5-HTP.) Or St. John's wort (300 mg): 1–3 at lunch; 1–3 at dinner; 1 at bedtime. Or SAM-e (400 mg): 2 at breakfast; 2 at lunch. (If you get no improvement after one bottle, discontinue.)

    Need: Sleep

    Recommendation: Melatonin (1–6 mg) at bedtime.

- *For depression with sensitivity*
    Need: Comfort
    Recommendation: DLPA (500 mg)
    1–2 capsules 3 times a day. Free-form amino acid blend (700–800 mg), 1–2 capsules morning and midmorning. (You probably won't need the complete amino blend after the first month if you're eating plenty of protein three times a day.)

- *For depression with stress*
    Need: Relaxation
    Recommendation: GABA (100–500 mg)
    1–3 times a day at or before your high-stress times, or try a combination of GABA with the aminos taurine and glycosine or inositol (such as GABA Calm by Source Naturals, True Calm by Now Foods, or Amino Relaxers by Country Life).

If you're under stress and have adrenal overload, it is common to fight cravings as well. For excessive sweet and starch cravings, try glutamine 500 (1500 mg), early morning, midmorning, midafternoon, and at bedtime, if you tend to wake up hungry in the night. Also, take chromium (200 mcg), 3 times per day with meals and at bedtime.

4. Take medication.

Dr. Daniel Amen has isolated seven types of depression, based on his years working with SPECT scans and treating clients. He has graciously given me permission to share the following with you, which includes any medications he might prescribe in situations where supplements, exercise, and other natural cures are not working—or in cases of severe depression, which we never take lightly. (As you saw from Tina Zahn's story, clinical depression is an emergency situation, and we do all we can to "stop the bleeding" with the best medications we have. Once we are no longer worried that our clients are suicidal, we can work with them to taper off of antidepressants and onto lifestyle changes that may prove to be enough.)

The following information is summarized from *Healing Anxiety and*

Depression by Daniel G. Amen and Lisa C. Routh. It is an excellent resource should you want to dive into more information.[6]

- *Type 1. Pure anxiety*

  Symptoms: Sufferers with this type feel stirred up, anxious, or nervous.

  SPECT: Increased activity in the basal ganglia, seen on both the concentration and baseline studies

  Medications: Buspar, short-term use of benzodiazepines

- *Type 2. Pure depression*

  Symptoms: This type is associated with primary depressive symptoms that range from chronic mild sadness (termed *dysthymia*) to the devastating illness of major depression. The hallmark symptoms of "pure depression" include: a persistent sad or negative mood; a loss of interest in usually pleasurable activities; periods of crying; frequent feelings of guilt, helplessness, hopelessness, or worthlessness; sleep and appetite changes (too much or too little); low energy levels; suicidal thoughts or attempts; and low self-esteem.

  SPECT: Markedly increased activity in the deep limbic area at rest and during concentration, and decreased prefrontal cortex at rest that improves with concentration. Deactivation of the prefrontal cortex at rest and improvement with concentration is a finding that is very commonly, but not always, present.

  Medications: Stimulating antidepressants such as Wellbutrin

- *Type 3. Mixed anxiety and depression*

  Symptoms: Sufferers of this type have a combination of both pure anxiety symptoms and pure depressive symptoms.

  SPECT: Excessive activity in the brain's basal ganglia and deep limbic system

  Medications: Antidepressants with antianxiety qualities, such as desipramine

- *Type 4. Overfocused anxiety and depression*

    Symptoms: These people have trouble shifting attention and tend to get locked into negative thoughts or behaviors.

    SPECT: Increased cingulate gyrus activity and increased basal ganglia and/or deep limbic activity at rest and during concentration

    Medications: SSRI antidepressants

- *Type 5. Temporal lobe anxiety and depression*

    Symptoms: When there are problems in this part of the brain, people struggle with temper outbursts; memory problems; mood instability; visual or auditory illusions; and dark, frightening, or evil thoughts. People with this type tend to misinterpret comments as negative when they are not, have trouble reading social situations, and appear to have mild paranoia. There may be a family history of these problems, or they can be triggered by a brain injury.

    SPECT: Increased or decreased activity in the temporal lobes and increased basal ganglia and/or deep limbic activity at rest and during concentration

    Medications: Antiseizure medications

- *Type 6. Cyclic anxiety and depression*

    Symptoms: Cyclic disorders, such as bipolar disorder, cyclothymia, and premenstrual tension syndrome, along with panic attacks, fit in this category because they are episodic and unpredictable. The hallmark of this type is its cyclical nature.

    SPECT: Not surprisingly, SPECT scan findings vary with the phase of the illness or the point in the patient's cycle. For example, when someone is in a manic phase of a bipolar illness, there is increased deep limbic activity and what we call "patchy uptake"—which means there are multiple hot spots of overactivity throughout the brain. When this same person is in a depressed state, there is overactivity in the limbic area, but not the patchy look of hot spots all over the scan.

    Medications: Antiseizure medications or Lithium for bipolar disorder; full-spectrum lights for seasonal affective disorder

- *Type 7. Low anxiety and depression*

   Symptoms: This type complains of being inattentive, distracted, bored, off task, and impulsive. The problem may also be the result of some form of toxic exposure or brain infection, such as chronic fatigue syndrome, a near-drowning accident, or other insults to the brain.

   SPECT: Decreased activity in the prefrontal cortex at rest and during concentration, along with increased basal ganglia and/or deep limbic activity; sometimes overall decreased activity

   Medications: Wellbutrin, Provigil, stimulant medications (such as Adderall, Concerta, Ritalin, or Dexedrine)

Knowing your type is essential to getting the right help for yourself.

5. Let there be light! "Light is sweet, and it pleases the eyes to see the sun" (Eccl. 11:7 NIV).

More than 25 percent of Americans suffer from a special sensitivity to the natural decrease in sunlight during the fall and winter in a condition called SAD (or seasonal affective disorder). For many lower-serotonin people, late afternoon brings on the sad hours. If you are able to get to a window, open up your curtains first thing in the morning and let the sunshine in. It will help your emotional outlook on the day and also help you sleep better at night. Research is showing that we may have overcompensated in our fear of skin cancer by keeping people from getting the sun they need for vitamin D production. Ten to fifteen minutes a day out in the sun is good for our moods and our health.

Getting some natural sunlight will be a big boost. Even on a cloudy day you'll get 10,000 times more lux (the standard unit of illumination) outdoors than you'll get indoors. There are special therapeutic lamps that you can sit under for several minutes a day if needed.

Note: Bright lights can also trigger irritable or manic moods. If major mood swings or bipolar moods are a condition for you, avoid these lamps.

You can buy full-spectrum lamps in a variety of models, of just purchase the bulbs from a health or hardware store. ParaLite, Verilux, Happy Eyes, and OttLite are a sampling of the brand names you can search.

6. Laugh! It's a wonderful mood lightener.

One of the comments I loved hearing from people who read my first book, *This Is Your Brain on Joy,* is that simply the process of reading the book seemed to have an antidepressant effect. They often mentioned the light and cheerful tone, my sense of humor (however weak it may be at times), and the stories I told on myself. I have to admit that the process of researching and writing about the topic of joy must have elevated my neurotransmitters because I had such a blast writing that book. And even now, if I'm down, I can pick it up and read a little and feel more cheerful.

Humor and laughter are amazingly uplifting to the mind and body. Consider, for example:

- Laughter expands blood vessels and sends more blood to the rest of your body. A good bout of laughter also reduces the levels of stress hormones epinephrine and cortisol. It can be said to be a form of dynamic meditation or relaxation.
- Researchers have found that after laughter there is an increase in antibodies in the mucous of the nose and respiratory passages, which is believed to have protective capacity against some viruses, bacteria, and other microorganisms.
- Laughter increases the levels of endorphins in our bodies, which are natural painkillers.
- Laughter is one of the best exercises for improving lung capacity and oxygen levels in the blood.

Funny writers such as the late Erma Bombeck, Bill Cosby, Paul Reiser, and Dave Barry can be good for what ails you on a blue day. And of course, there's no one quite like Garrison Keillor to make even the most stoic Minnesota Lutheran crack a smile. Going to see a funny movie or play, reading the "funny papers," or signing up for a Laugh-a-Day via e-mail are all wonderful ways to lift the spirits and get you off sad or looping negative thoughts.

Hang out as often as possible with friends who make you laugh. And if you've married a funny spouse, thank him or her for adding years to your life and smiles to your miles. Joanne Woodward, happily married to Paul

Newman for decades, said, "Sexiness wears thin after a while, and good looks fade. But to be married to a man who makes you laugh every day? Now *that's* a treat."[7]

7. Make love with your spouse any way you can, as soon as you can.

Did you know that most couples who make love often and regularly usually begin making advances toward each other before both of them *feel* like it? The ol' pros know that "if you build it" the feelings will come. Making love often is really like riding a bike: the more you do it, the easier it is. And having healthy regular sex will contribute as much to your happiness and health as any pill in a bottle. It really operates on the "use it or lose it" principle. Though, admittedly, as men get a little older, it takes an extra day or so to get fully reloaded. Still, there is no reason a couple in their fifties can't enjoy lusty liaisons two to three times a week if they'd like to. (Two great supplements for male virility are ginkgo and l-arginine.)

One friend of mine in her twenties, who enjoys a fabulous sex life with her husband, said, "I grew up with parents who flirted and let us kids know they enjoyed their sex life in a natural and wonderful way. If Mom got grumpy, Dad would say, 'Carla, I think you need some "medicine."' And off they'd go to their bedroom for a good while. Mom always came out smiling, so I figured that whatever they did in there was good for her. In fact, when we were too little to realize what they were up to, and Mom was in a bad mood, I remember my little brother saying, 'Dad, I think you'd better give Mom her medicine now.' My parents broke out laughing."

I think sex is the glue God gave couples to bring them together regularly and connect them emotionally. The hormones released during sex are both calming and bonding for the man and the woman. In addition, frequent sex and orgasms with a loving spouse translates into lower death rates and lower risk of heart attacks for both men and women.

- Health benefits for men and women are rather telling. According to a study of men who are sexual two times a week or more, there is a 50 percent drop in mortality from heart attacks. There is no heart health program in the medical community that has proven to be as effective. Women also have a drop in mortality rates from heart attacks based on quality rather than frequency of sexual experience.

In other words, lousy sexual experiences shorten a woman's life span. Lack of sexual frequency shortens a man's life span. So if couples want to live longer, it pays to be interested in both quality and frequency of their love life.[8]

- Dr. Ted McIlvenna, president of the Institute for Advanced Study of Human Sexuality, found that sexually active people draw far more joy from their lives than others. They also take fewer sick leaves, which should please every employer.[9]
- Gynecologist Dudley Chapman contended that orgasms help the body fight infections, a proposition supported by psychologists from Wilkes University.[10]
- More recently, a study conducted in Melbourne, Australia, found that frequent ejaculation between the ages of twenty and fifty helps dramatically decrease the risk of prostate cancer in men. This study ties with other research and suggests that regular orgasm in males prevents painful urination in old age.[11]
- There are some studies that indicate that the sperm of a man in a woman has antidepressant effects on her mood.

Also, keep in mind that there are dozens of ways to make love without ever having sex. Keeping the flirting simmering on the days you don't have sex is wonderful for increasing the joy in your life. Here are a few ways to seduce your lover, whether or not you make love:

- Gaze at your wife and tell her why you love her.
- Give your mate a back rub.
- Snuggle up to watch TV together.
- Pat your spouse on the behind, and tell him what a stud he is.
- Stay awake for some pillow talk.
- Pray for your mate when he or she is down.
- Wives, wear something that you know will drive him wild when it's just you two at home.

- Flirt by e-mail or texting.
- Give each other a ten-second kiss.

8. Create a bright mood environment.

Begin to put some serious thought into your happiness. Mentally go through your day and jot down how you can upsize the joy in everything you do. (*This Is Your Brain on Joy* is full of ideas.) For example, while you are getting ready for work, could you put some music on to brush your teeth by? Are there "happy fragrances" to get you going in the morning? Citrus fragrances are great for waking up the prefrontal cortex.

Becky, my friend and collaborator for this book, says, "I am not a morning person and, for some reason, tend to wake up in a bit of a low mood. I love natural lemon smells, so I keep a jar of C. O. Bigelow lemon balm in my nightstand to slather on my hands and to put on my lips as soon as I open my eyes. Waking up to these happy scents I love makes mornings a little easier for me. Then I take some focusing amino acids— like tyrosine or DPLA—with water that I keep nearby as well. I like amino acids because you can take them on an empty stomach without any tummy upset. In a few minutes I can feel my brain snap, cracklin' and poppin', and I have the energy to get out of bed. Then as soon as I get up, I stand at the window and let the sunshine in on my face.

"I used to stumble toward the coffeepot, but have found that beginning my day with a smoothie made of frozen banana, milk, berries, and protein powder is a far superior energy booster and is just fabulous for digestion. Another pick-me-up concoction I love on hot days is 'green lemonade'—a good squeeze of fresh lemon, a teaspoon of a green food powder (found in health food stores), a dash of agave nectar or stevia to sweeten, and a teaspoon of liquid l-carnatine by Now products, in citrus flavor. (This brand of liquid carnatine is a yummy-tasting supplement in and of itself.) Stir well, add about a cup of water and ice, stir again, and enjoy! My college-age son loves this and makes a glass before work or school. Tasty! Coffee seemed to be hard on my stomach and also my blood pressure. Sometimes if I miss the taste of coffee, I'll put a little of my husband's brew in my smoothie and make a mocha. Or try rooibos tea, which has more antioxidants than green tea; made into a tea latte, with the addition of warm milk and agave nectar, it is fabulous on cold mornings. I try to read something inspirational and short as I sip my smoothie. And on my best days, I'll walk or exercise before the day assaults me and I've put working out on the back burner again."

Think about colors as mood and energy boosters or chill-out helpers. Using soft lime greens or yellows will wake you up and are great colors for a workout room, kitchen, or office—or a dark basement that needs light. Blues and creams promote a calm, happy, restful feeling and are great for bedrooms.

Walk mentally through your day and ask yourself, *What can I do to increase the joy coming into my senses? What smells can I add? What music lifts my mood? What inspirational literature or scriptures can I read? Where can I increase light? What tastes wake up my mouth and make my body feel clean and energized? Can I stretch or walk or dance before diving into brain work? Is there a supplement I can take that will feed my brain and help it make happy neurotransmitters? Can I hug, kiss, or shower with my spouse?* Pay attention to the feel of clothing and ask what fabrics you find yourself feeling happiest in. When you buy clothes, look at the color and style, but pay much attention to how they feel on you, because we all end up wearing clothes that feel best next to our skin. A dozen little pleasures can add a big boost of joy to your day.

9. Get your beauty "treatments."

People who work and live around beauty, not surprisingly, tend to be happier. If you can live in Hawaii or the mountains of Colorado, do it! But most of us have to create our own beauty in the backyard where we live. You need a little bit of Eden both outside and inside your home—and even in your cubicle at work.

Lots of people enjoy planting a flower garden or a few potted flowers in their backyards. Add a porch swing, hammock, or lounge chair nearby, with a little table . . . so that you can sip your morning tea with the birds, and you've got your own little piece of heaven. Or perhaps you like fish ponds or fountains or an herb or veggie garden where you can enjoy the beauty and also have a pretty place to tinker. Even if you just grow a little bit of mint or basil or cherry tomatoes, there's nothing like growing something you get to look at, eat, and enjoy.

Also, create a sacred spot or space in your home where you can go to simply rest and be refreshed. I like to call these *Eden spots*. One friend of mine loves her bubble baths—with lavender oil and Epsom salts, candles, and music. Another guy friend of mine has a comfy chair where he sips his morning cup o' joe while reading the paper and his Bible. Keep your sacred spot beautiful, however you see beauty. Maybe you'll want a basket of uplifting or funny books, a Bible, notebook, a bottle of water, and great gel pen nearby. If your spot is on a chair, chaise, or couch, then a soft throw is also nice, along with a pillow or two. A music source is a plus or an iPod or CD player with uplifting talks, scriptures, or comic routines. When you feel sad or stressed, just tell your family, "I'm going to my Eden spot for a few minutes. I'll come back happier."

10. Remember, your glasses are foggy and dark.

Try to remember that when you are depressed or in a low mood, your mind will automatically go on a "mental garbage hunt," dredging up the saddest and worst memories of your loved ones from your past. You are not seeing people in their best light, not even in shades of black and white, but in real depression you are experiencing others through the darkest colored glasses from the worst possible eye view.

What you feel versus what is true can be very skewed in a low-mood state. Many marriages do not survive a depression sleeping between them because of this very reason. From your viewpoint, your mate may seem to be unable to do much of anything right, to say anything helpful, to do or be who you need him or her to be. Even the way he chews may irritate you. True, he probably *doesn't* understand how you feel, because he may never have survived a dark night of the soul such as you may experience in a deep depression. Just recognizing that your mate is probably doing his best and allowing *him* to help *you* get the help you need is the most important thing you can do.

Withhold any decisions, any grand declarations, or major changes— especially in your marriage—until you are sure that your chemicals are firing correctly. Yes, if you are in a truly abusive or neglectful marriage, these circumstances can certainly make you depressed. But if you know that your mate is a good man or a good woman who loves you and is trying his or her best, then your negative feelings about him or her truly could be stemming from neurochemistry rather than a bad marriage. You owe it to yourself to find out.

TEN TIPS TO HELP
YOUR BLUE MOOD MATE

1. Give a hand.

Read through the above list and do all you can to help your depressed mate to eat well, take supplements, and enjoy uplifting or humorous movies, books, and friends. Open windows, and encourage sitting outside when the weather permits. Sunshine is helpful. For a depressed person, the most difficult thing about the above list is how overwhelming it all seems. The smallest changes may seem huge. You can help by encouraging your mate to take one positive step at a time, doing one small joy-booster here and another one there.

2. Get him or her to someone who can help.

Do the research yourself and drive your low-mood lover to a health practitioner whom you feel will be of real help. On Dr. Amen's Web site—www .amenclinics.com—there is a list of therapists and doctors who understand brain balancing and can work with you accordingly. If the low mood is mild or seasonal, you may find some of the help you need from the local health food store; many have knowledgeable nutritionists on staff.

3. Become informed.

Reading this book and my first book, *This Is Your Brain on Joy,* are great places to start getting informed about not only depression but how other parts of the brain can lead to a variety of kinds of depression. Dr. Amen's book *Healing Anxiety and Depression*, *The Mood Cure* by Julia Ross, and *Natural Highs* by Dr. Hyla Cass and Patrick Holford are particularly helpful in understanding how amino acids work to relieve depression.

4. Don't use God to beat up your mate.

Do not say anything to compound your mate's pain by spiritualizing or guilting her for being down. The worst thing you can say is, "A healthy Christian shouldn't feel this way." Or, "God loves you and you know it, so get over it!" A kinder approach would be to point out the up-and-down moods of the psalmist David. Point out that Jesus understands and was "acquainted with sorrow." Ask if she'd like you to pray for her, but don't assume she wants this. Remember the dark and foggy glasses through which she is seeing the world? She is also seeing God in shades of gray right now. Love her with your actions and a little less through words, until she is better able to receive the "good news" you are trying to share.

5. Take good care of you.

Depression can be "catching," so make sure you are putting the oxygen over your own face first, so to speak, before trying to rescue your spouse. You do not want to diminish your joy or your fun when caring for a partner who is depressed. Leave him at home with a funny movie and a nutritious meal now and then—and take a night off to enjoy yourself and replenish your spirit. You will need to have a full tank of joy to handle the drain of living with a depressed mate . . . until he is better.

6. Learn the art of "being present."

While a depressed person is recovering, ask how you can help. Some people need you to hold them while they cry and find a good deal of relief after letting out the tears. Do not be afraid of just being with your mate in this time of sorrow and silently holding her, stroking her hair, or whispering words of love. Counselors have to learn how to detach from their clients' pain while still being compassionate witnesses to their suffering. You can learn this skill too. You can hold people and comfort those who are sad without going to the depths with them. Henri Nouwen wrote, "The friend who can be silent with us in a moment of despair or confusion, who can stay with us in an hour of grief and bereavement, who can tolerate not knowing . . . not healing, not curing . . . that is a friend who cares."[12]

7. Listen deeply.

I saw a book the other day with the title *Listening Is an Act of Love*. As a therapist who listens to people all day long for a living, I had to agree with that premise. Many troubled souls have received comfort and cheer simply from being with a friend, counselor, or pastor who lets them unburden their thoughts. You don't have to fix anything or have all the answers. Just listen without judging or fixing, with compassion. Say things like, "I am so sorry you are in so much pain. I know you have lots of inner strength and that you'll move through this and find a way to feel better. And I'll be here with you. It's going to be okay. I love you."

8. Don't try too hard to cheer her up.

Subtlety is key when people are down. The last thing they want is a bouncy, cheerful, happy clown to try to make them smile. They need your gentle understanding first of all. Then think about how you might upsize the joy in their physical environment without making it obvious or being loud and obnoxious about it.

Rather than saying, "Get up, Grumpy! Let's go for a run in the fresh air! Or how about we go see a funny movie? I've got to get you out of the dumps!"—go for subtler approaches.

Perhaps, just open the curtains and let in some light. Or say, "I've made us some smoothies; would you like to sip them outside in the sun with me for a few minutes?" Maybe turn on some music that you know she enjoys or light a candle with a scent she loves. As you are sipping smoothies, smile softly and, naturally and calmly, tell them an interesting or funny thing that happened to you or something light that you read. Maybe ask, "What was the funniest thing that ever happened to you?" or "What part of a movie made you laugh the hardest?" Take a bowl of peas or pecans outside with you to shell together. (Remember that simply moving your hands helps perk up your brain.) As you see her mood lifting and her energy rising, you might say, "Would you like to just take a short stroll around the block? Maybe five or ten minutes?"

Inch by inch, gently lead those who are in darkness to light. But do not whack them over the head with a joy stick.

9. *Reassure him that he isn't alone—and he will get better.*

Share stories of famous people who went through depressions and made it to the other side. If your husband is an athlete, you will want to share a few sports hero stories of overcoming depression. If he is in ministry, share stories of saints who suffered with low moods and came through it. Just Google "famous depressed people" and be prepared to be amazed at the long and varied list.

10. *Help, but don't enable.*

Parents of well-adjusted physically or mentally challenged children know that they are loving their children best by helping them with things they can't do—but never doing things that they know their children can and should do or try to do for themselves. In a similar way, you want to help your mate do what he or she cannot do, but don't fall into the trap of babying or enabling a prolonged depression.

One way to do this is to be a noticer and a bit of an armchair therapist. Notice the times when your mate seems to find the energy to accomplish tasks or go out in the world.

One husband noticed that when his wife had nothing planned to do during the day, she would stay in bed and sink into a funk. The house would be a mess, and she could not muster the energy to begin to clean it. Oddly enough, when she had a lunch planned with a friend, or took her child to a playgroup, or took a class at the local YMCA, she seemed to get *more* done on the house. Once she started moving, the energy to clean the house, do laundry, and cook dinner seemed to come.

So, together, they came up with a daily schedule and made sure she had something to do, outside of the house—some appointment, some friend to meet, some art or exercise class to take—every single day. Never underestimate the power of "something to look forward to" to get the happy juices flowing.

Little by little, more energy to do life came back to his wife.

Happiness is usually not terribly complicated. It generally comes to us when we have someone to love who loves us back, something worthwhile for the hands to do, something special to look forward to, and a deep knowing that God loves us. There is much to be said for old-fashioned ways to beat the blues. However, when the simple things, such as sunshine, good food, honest work, and love aren't doing the trick, I'm thankful that we have brain science to help ourselves and our marriages back to the sunny side of life's street.

Please rate yourself on each of the symptoms listed below, using the following scale:

0=Never 1=Rarely 2=Occasionally 3=Frequently 4=Very Frequently
N/A=Not Applicable/Not Known
    (You answer in one column, your mate in the other column.)

____ ____   1. Short fuse or periods of extreme irritability

____ ____   2. Periods of rage with little provocation

____ ____   3. Often misinterprets comments as negative when they are not

____ ____   4. Irritability tends to build, then explodes, then recedes; often tired after a rage

____ ____   5. Periods of spaciness or confusion

____ ____   6. Periods of panic and/or fear for no specific reason

____ ____   7. Visual or auditory changes, such as seeing shadows or hearing muffled sounds

____ ____   8. Frequent periods of déjà vu (feelings of being somewhere you have never been)

____ ____   9. Sensitivity or mild paranoia

____ ____ 10. Headaches or abdominal pain of uncertain origin

____ ____ 11. History of a head injury or family history of violence or explosiveness

____ ____ 12. Dark thoughts, may involve suicidal or homicidal thoughts

____ ____ 13. Periods of forgetfulness or memory problems

Results: If there are five or more symptoms at a level 3 or 4, you may have temporal lobe overactivity or underactivity. In my personal experience over the past ten years, 100 percent of people scanned have had temporal lobe overactivity or underactivity in either or both the left and right temporal lobes. Those people may struggle with mood swings—times of high energy or mania that may shift suddenly to dark depressions or volatility.

From Amen Brain Subsystem Checklist, used by permission from Dr. Daniel Amen and the Amen Clinic.

CHAPTER SEVEN

The Agitated Lover
(Temporal Lobes)

Don't get even; get mad. Whatever else has been said about me personally is unimportant. When I sing, I believe. I'm honest.

—FRANK SINATRA

If you ever listened to "Fly Me to the Moon" or "You Make Me Feel So Young" or "I've Got You Under My Skin," you know that Ol' Blue Eyes, The Chairman of the Board, the leader of the Rat Pack . . . Frank Sinatra, knew his way around a love song—and not just to *his* generation. Watching him perform tender lyrics so effortlessly and sincerely in old black-and-white reruns is still a treat. Women still swoon when they hear Frankie belt out a tune, and men can't help but admire the amount of cool per square inch that was Sinatra, The Voice.

Which is why it is so hard, even disconcerting, to read about Frank—the man behind the stage presence of Sinatra, the singer. Talk about the epitome of a troubled soul . . . and living proof of the old adage that "hurting people hurt people." He hurt a lot of people who crossed his path when he was feeling, well, cross or crossed. I'd love to have been able to have had Mr. Sinatra's head examined via a SPECT scan. My guess is that I'd find some injury or malfunction in his temporal lobe (perhaps from a street fight when he was the tough kid from Hoboken).

Here's just a small sampling of Frank's legendary temper tantrums:

- For all of his life, Sinatra had a very unpredictable temper, often screaming at reporters and getting in fights. In one particularly

violent tantrum, he ripped a phone out of the wall of his hotel
room, broke the windows, and then set it on fire.

- He once had a helipad installed on his Palm Springs property for a
much-anticipated presidential visit. When JFK chose to stay with
Bing Crosby instead, Sinatra, in a fury, attacked the helipad with a
sledgehammer.
- When Peter Lawford declined an invitation to visit, Sinatra
shredded some of his clothes, which Lawford had left in the
guest-room closet, and threw them into his pool. On yet another
occasion he threw a woman through a plate-glass window, nearly
severing her arm.
- Sinatra also had a spat with casino manager Carl Cohen. When the
crooner doused him with hot coffee, Cohen slugged him in the
face, knocking out his two front teeth.

Frank was a man of many contradictions. He was fiercely loyal to and
protective of Sammy Davis Jr., during some of the worse times in our civil
rights history. He was often generous to those who were down on their luck
but would get an adrenaline rush from picking a fight with a stranger. His
love life was legendary and, ultimately, rocky and tragic. He was a friend of
presidents and had ties with the Mafia. He was a man of passions, and few
of them were ever contained, bridled, or channeled for long.

MUSIC TO CALM THE SAVAGE CROONER

Especially fascinating to me is the quote from Sinatra that I used to open this
chapter: "When I sing, I believe. I am honest." Indeed, I think Sinatra was
probably his best and most authentic self when he was singing. Unable to
find peace unless he was singing, he performed his last public concert when
he was eighty years old. Music was more than a career to Frankie; it was the
balm to the raging storm within and a lifeline to sanity. When the music
died, and he could no longer sing, Frank died soon after.

Though I can only speculate from what I've read and heard of Sinatra,
his behavior patterns are consistent with someone who has temporal lobe

problems, perhaps coupled with cingulate issues. Sinatra also drank heavily and when doing so would become increasingly violent or depressed. His anger was always simmering—it seemed—and was either expressed in aggression toward others or inwardly toward himself in despondency. The alcohol only made things worse, taking his prefrontal cortex off-line and allowing his impulses to rule his actions.[1]

Here are a few common traits of someone with temporal lobe problems, and from reading about the life of Frank Sinatra, it is easy to see that he struggled with several of these issues, though not all of them.

- Has periods of quick temper or rages with little provocation
- Misinterprets comments as negative when they are not (chip on his or her shoulder the size of a boulder)
- Has a tendency to become increasingly irritable, then explodes, then recedes, and is often tired after a rage
- Has periods of spaciness or confusion
- Has periods of panic and/or fear for no specific reason
- Imagines visual changes, such as seeing shadows or objects changing shape
- Has frequent periods of déjà vu (feelings of being somewhere before even though he or she has never been there)
- Is supersensitive or mildly paranoid
- Experiences headaches or abdominal pain of uncertain origin
- Has a history of a head injury or family history of violence or explosiveness
- Has dark thoughts, may involve suicidal or homicidal issues
- Has periods of forgetfulness
- Has short fuse or periods of extreme irritability
- Has religious preoccupations or compulsions

Aggressiveness is the trait I see most often manifested when someone has a temporal lobe problem. In fact, in a large study performed by the Amen Clinic on people who had assaulted another person or damaged property, more than 70 percent had left temporal lobe abnormalities. One patient of Dr. Amen's with temporal lobe dysfunction (probably inherited in this case, since the man's father was a rage-aholic) complained of frequent violent, intense thoughts. He felt shame about them and didn't understand where they came from. "I can be walking down the street," he said, "and someone accidentally brushes against me, and I get the thoughts of wanting to shoot him or club him to death. These thoughts frighten me." Another woman spoke of accidentally bumping into someone and then suddenly raging at her. (It turned out that this woman had fallen off of a bunk bed at age four, damaging her temporal lobe.)

We also often see patients who have suicidal thoughts stemming from temporal lobe dysfunction. Bad thoughts of shame or of destroying oneself often come from temporal lobe problems. Typically, we see that left temporal lobe abnormalities produce more outward aggression, such as anger or irritability, and right temporal lobe problems are more associated with shame and anger turned inward.

Interestingly, one of the ways that temporal lobe function can be improved is by the use of music. Perhaps you recall the Old Testament story of King Saul, who struggled with bouts of rage and melancholy. But when David played the harp, Saul's demons left him and he calmed to the soothing music. I cannot help but wonder if while Sinatra was singing and was surrounded by music, his inner demons settled and calmed. "When I sing, I believe," Sinatra said. I wonder what he was able to believe *in* when he sang, that perhaps he could not believe as easily when he wasn't immersed in music. Did he believe in love, in God, in joy, and in peace? Was there a window of calm as he sang that was like Prozac to his soul? Perhaps when Sinatra sang, his brain balanced and got closer to the brain he was meant to have—the "Eden Brain"—and in those moments, he experienced the goodness of God, the beauty of love, and his audience felt this magic moment with him. The temporal lobes "allow us to be stimulated, relaxed, or brought to ecstasy by the experience of great music," says Dr. Amen.[2]

But when the curtain dropped and the stage lights dimmed, the dark thoughts would move in and Sinatra would be on the hunt for another kind of medication or fix to make the thoughts go away: Jack Daniel's, or a woman to chase, or a fight to pick. During Sinatra's traumatic love affair with Ava Gardner, he reportedly tried to commit suicide twice. Ava appeared to have shared many of Sinatra's vices: lack of impulse control, alcoholism, and addiction to adrenaline highs. Their addictive brand of love was a match made in Crazy Land.

An aside here: Several years ago I was testifying in a medical malpractice trial in London, England. I took a long walk one evening to see the sights in London, and took one of the famous black cabs back to my hotel. When the friendly elderly cabbie dropped me off at my hotel, he got out of the cab, pointed across the street and said, "See that building over there?" I nodded. "It was used as a USO club back in World War II. One night I was parked in this very same spot, behind a line of trucks filled with food to be distributed among the citizens here. Suddenly, out of that door burst Frank Sinatra and Ava Gardner yelling and screaming at each other. She seemed tired of arguing, took off a large diamond ring, and threw it into the bushes. The truck drivers all laughed and cheered her as they watched Frank Sinatra switch from rage to panic as he went on a diving expedition into the shrubbery searching for that diamond ring!"

Alas, movie stars do not have the corner on roller-coaster drama, aggression, and anger-plagued marriages. Temporal lobe imbalances happen to everyday folks, turning their marriages into soap opera–like stories.

WHAT'S A TEMPORAL LOBE?

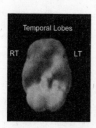

The temporal lobes house a wide variety of functions, making them among the more complicated mood centers to pinpoint and describe. They are housed on either side of the brain, near the temples and ears, and look a little like the thumb on a baseball glove. At one time scientists thought the temporal lobes were little more than "armrests" for the brain, but we've discovered they are some of the richest parts of the brain's anatomy. Our deepest memories are held here. They are also the artsy parts of the brain as well as the "temper lofts" because music, spirituality, literature, rhythm, language, tones, and memory are processed here. Here's a list of the healthy versus unhealthy functions of the temporal lobe:

Healthy Temporal Lobe Functions	Unhealthy Temporal Lobe Problems
Understanding/use of language	Learning problems
Auditory learning	Auditory and visual processing problems
Retrieval of words	Trouble finding the right word
Emotional stability	Mood instability
Facilitating long-term memory	Memory problems
Reading (left side)	Aggression toward self or others
Reading faces	Trouble reading facial expressions or social cues
Reading social cues (right side)	Anxiety for little or no reason
Verbal intonation	Headaches or abdominal pain, hard to diagnose
Rhythm, music	Overfocused on religious ideas
Visual learning	Illusions (shadows, visual or auditory distortions)
Spiritual experience	Dark, evil, awful, or hopeless thoughts

Problems with Low Activity in the Temporal Lobe (will show up as dents in the surface scans, looking like tie-dyed bread dough) Head injury is a common cause of temporal lobe issues.

- Anxiety amnesia
- Left side: aggression, dyslexia
- Right side: trouble with social cues
- Dissociation
- Temporal epilepsy
- Serious depression with dark or suicidal thoughts

Problems with High Activity in the Temporal Lobe (will show up as overlit areas of the brain in the active scan)

- Epilepsy
- Religiosity
- Increased intuition or sensory perception

In marriage counseling, I use the following chart as a simple way to show what temporal lobe problems look like in a day-to-day relationship:

Healthy Temporal Lobes	Unstable Temporal Lobes
Process tone of voice consistently with the other person's intentions	Will genuinely hear others as angry or critical when they are not
Accurately process facial expressions	Tendency to overinterpret or underinterpret facial expressions; have difficulty reading social cues
Manage anger, irritability, or frustration	Anger can quickly escalate out of control. There is the feeling of "walking on pins and needles" for those who live or work with someone with temporal lobe imbalances.
Able to access short-term memory and long-term memory under times of stress	Have difficulty accessing memory under stress, whether it is short-term or long-term
May feel depressed, irritated, or hopeless, but can work through it	Frustration, depression, irritation can turn into thoughts of harming self and others.

WHEN BAD BRAINS HAPPEN TO GOOD MARRIAGES

There are some great books on how to manage anger, and even the hilarious movie *Anger Management* has a few helpful tips for the calm-impaired. But what do you do when your collection of anger-management books begins filling up faster than the "improving your love life" shelf?

This is exactly how Al explained his predicament when he came into my office holding a copy of his brain scan, hoping that there would be answers for his decades of futility trying to beat his tendency toward explosive anger. No matter what he read, how often he counted to ten, or told himself to be calm, eventually, inevitably, Al would gradually end up in the same spot of lecturing or exploding at the woman he loved and with whom he wanted to spend his life.

Only now, the love of his life, Lori, wanted to end their marriage. She'd grown tired of listening to promises that he would change, that he would not raise his voice, intimidate, or threaten her again. Numb from the years of anger that had permeated their life together, and with their two children grown and out of the house, she was ready to make her escape. She knew the kids would be shocked at first when hearing the news that their mother was finally filing for divorce, but she also knew they would understand. In fact, Lori was pretty sure that she would actually see more of her adult kids and her future grandchildren if she could create a safe haven for all of them, away from the walking-on-eggshells environment they'd all lived in for so many years.

Al had somehow talked Lori into coming with him for this visit with me. She reluctantly agreed but made a promise to herself that this was it, the final effort she would make. She was, as she explained, "All out of *try*." On one hand, inwardly she hoped against hope that maybe, just maybe, the scan in her husband's hand would help unlock the mystery of his anger. On the other hand, she dared not hope. Lori took mental note of the countless hours of therapy, Christian books that promised her that "submission" was the key to marital happiness, only to discover that submission meant submitting to verbal abuse and ultimately giving in to Al's sexual demands, which made her feel used and demeaned instead of loved or cherished. "Making love," when her heart had been broken so many times by the barrage of his anger, only created more inner numbness . . . more disconnection . . . waiting for it to be over with, so he would leave her alone.

Lori slowly lowered herself into a chair as Al handed me the scan. I brought this image up on the monitor on my desk. Compassion welled up as I surveyed the damage to Al's temporal lobes.

 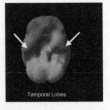

Al's temporal lobe brain versus normal brain

Al was physically abused by his father when he was growing up. The injury that he received in the right frontal and temporal lobe happened when he yelled at his father for raging at his mother. His father quickly turned from yelling at Al's mother and threw one punch that knocked his son out. He then proceeded to kick Al in the stomach and head. The screams of his mother and sisters somehow reached his father, who then finally stopped the beating. Al did not remember much of what had happened. He learned the facts from his sisters and from later looking at old medical charts from the hospital where he was taken that long-ago, traumatic night.

Al's injury was so great that he genuinely could not tell how angry he would get when under stress, nor could he comprehend the impact of his words on his spouse and children.

Lori began to cry as I explained the source of the inexplicable and volatile anger all these years. Her tears were for herself, her children, grandchildren, and her husband. For years lost because they just didn't know. Now, here was the answer. Finally.

Tragically, the consequences of those years of hurt were still there to work through. Did she have enough compassion left in her bruised heart to reach back toward Al? With her husband's brain scan on the screen, comprehending what it meant, and with the assurance I gave her that we could help . . . hope began to gingerly float once more.

I explained to Al that he was 100 percent responsible, now that he had this information, to care for his brain so he could break the patterns of rage. He agreed to start on a mood stabilizer called Trileptal, which is a great medication for stabilizing the temporal lobes. Once his temporal lobes were calmed, he also began to take an antidepressant to help his low-mood states and also to help knock that overfocused, controlling gerbil off the wheel of his cingulate gyrus.

The change was nothing short of miraculous. Although people with temporal lobe issues can be some of the worst spouses because of the horrible effects of unbridled rage on their mates, when their brains are calmed—most effectively by medication—it's as though this wonderful person suddenly joins the marriage, or the family. Medication isn't always needed, but when it is, as in Al's case, it can be like a miracle, allowing people to be their truest selves, many times for the first time in decades.

NOTE: RESPONSIBILITY IS A TWO-SIDED COIN

No one escapes the consequences of his or her actions. Al is responsible for loving his brain, caring for it, and learning about it so that he no longer allows his anger to have free rein, inflicting more pain on his wife and children. (Author Susan Isaacs said that her father's angry outbursts, even cussing at the sports team on TV, felt like she was getting a painful electric shock to her brain with his every profane explosion. I think she speaks for most families who live with an intermittent "rager.")[3]

That said, as Al does take medication and changes (and often the results are pretty remarkable, pretty quickly), Lori now has the responsibility to let go of old (often buried) anger and resentment from the past in a healthy way. She's got to let her husband break out of the label of being "the angry husband" and give him space to become a changed man. Oftentimes we will find that spouses of the angry person, similar to spouses of addicted wives or husbands, have found their identity in being the "suffering saint" or martyr. Without the perks of that role, they feel a little lost. Or maybe, now that they feel safe, old feelings of anger that they had tamped down start to surface. All this to say, *both* spouses will have some adjusting to do; as one gets healthier, so the other is also forced to become healthier. Many times it isn't just the agitated lover who needs some brain balancing, but often his or her mate may need a few brain adjustments as well. A good marriage therapist who is familiar with brain issues can be especially helpful in this fragile transition time.

THREE KINDS OF ANGER

Though we know that aggressive behavior, including easily provoked anger and rage, along with verbal or physical abuse, is a temporal lobe problem, there is no way to know this for sure without a SPECT scan. Therefore, in order to treat the issues with pinpoint accuracy, I nearly always prefer that clients get a scan—particularly if there was a brain injury of any kind in their distant or recent past. Because the temporal lobes are housed in a little cup made of bony ridges in the skull, they are especially prone to injury during a trauma to the head when the tofulike temporal lobes hit the bony ridges.

The Amen Clinic's research has shown that these three different types of anger and violence all require different treatments. Knowing which type or combination of types is essential to getting the right help:

- Impulsive violence (low prefrontal cortex): Sudden and rash explosions; their "thinker" has left the building, and their emotions are suddenly in charge.
- Compulsive violence (high cingulate gyrus): This person gets stuck on a negative thought, cannot be dissuaded by internal logic, and grows angrier by the moment.
- Random or senseless violence (temporal lobe) accompanied by dark thoughts: This sort of rage is often accompanied by a deep sense of gloom, injustice, and self-righteousness if expressed in aggressive ways.

The SPECT scan can show us if one or more of the areas are affected; then we treat each area in a prescribed order. We always begin by balancing out the temporal lobes first with appropriate medication, if this area shows up on a scan as being under- or overactive. If you try to balance the cingulate first with an SSRI, you can actually make temporal lobe problems worse. Tragically, this happens in too many cases. A doctor or psychiatrist may prescribe an antidepressant to someone who complains of having dark or violent thoughts, and these are the people who you hear about in the news who "took Prozac and then committed suicide." If we suspect there is any possibility of a temporal lobe problem when doing the Amen Checklist, we do not recommend a SSRI until we are sure that the temporal lobes have been balanced first.

Other problems we've seen associated with over- or underactivity in the temporal lobes have to do with memory, hypergraphia (a tendency toward compulsive and extensive writing), and some have the opposite problem—difficulty getting the words out and on paper. Reading problems and interpreting social cues are also associated with temporal lobe imbalances.

RELIGIOUS PREOCCUPATION

If you've experienced the presence of God through prayer or when listening to music in church, it is most likely in the area of well-functioning temporal lobes where you sensed this connection. Some scientists have called this area "the God Spot" because of the experience of spiritual insight that often occurs in this part of the brain. It makes sense that God created us with brains that can experience and sense him. However, when the temporal lobes are not working correctly, a healthy experience of God can turn into a religious and decidedly unhealthy compulsion. The brilliant comic actor Gene Wilder (*Young Frankenstein, Willie Wonka and the Chocolate Factory*) shared in his memoir that as a young teen, he struggled with a terrible compulsion to pray for hours, sometimes into the wee hours of the night, for some generic but overwhelming feeling of guilt for crimes he could not name. He knew enough to know that this was not a normal prayer of someone who wanted to communicate with God but a compulsion, something terrible that he could not explain and yet could not stop.

Later in his life, he worked in a mental hospital and noticed that some of the patients had certain compulsions they could not stop. One man was terrified of stepping on a crack. Another prayed for hours in front of a TV set. At this point it occurred to Gene that perhaps he wasn't guilty for some terrible unknown sin—but was simply a little sick in the head. Over time, with the help of a therapist, Mr. Wilder realized that he developed the compulsion to pray for his sins when his mother became bedbound with a weak heart. At some level he felt responsible for her illness. In fact, the family doctor had warned him never to upset his mother or it might kill her—but to do everything he could to make her happy. During this frightening and fragile time, Gene also went to a school where he was regularly beaten by boys because he was Jewish. I do not know if he suffered any blows to the head that could have left him susceptible to temporal lobe issues—along with the trigger of his mother's illness—but his praying compulsion reminded me of some of the temporal lobe stories I've heard from the Amen Clinic.

Dr. Amen had a little boy in his practice who made himself physically sick by worrying about all the people who were going to hell. Another patient spent seven days a week in church, praying for the souls of his family. Another could not stop thinking about the mysteries of life long enough to actually live his life in a functional way.

TEN TIPS TO CALM THE AGITATED LOVER WITHIN

1. Have a SPECT scan first.

Because there is such a danger of prescribing medication that can make things worse rather than better, when I suspect a temporal lobe issue (as a result of the Amen Checklist questions), I will do all I can to help persuade the client to get a scan. There is just too much at risk on the table to play a guessing game with medication. A commonly prescribed stimulant or a typical antidepressant, either one, could make someone with temporal lobe issues much worse, perhaps even suicidal. You can understand why I urge my clients who may have temporal lobe issues to get a scan in order to have a pinpointed, accurate diagnosis.

2. Take medications.

Antiseizure meds for mood instability and temper problems are Depakote, Neurontin, Gabitril, Lamictal, Trileptal, and Topamax. Medications that are helpful with bipolar disorder are Lithium, Depakote, Trileptal, and Tegretol.

Neurontin and Lyrica are helpful for anxiety and for pain management. Gabitril is also helpful for anxiety.

Memory-enhancing meds for more serious memory problems are Namenda, Aricept, Exelon, or Reminyl. These medications are helpful for those whose memory problems are related to trauma and are often also used with Alzheimer's and various forms of dementia.

If there is a dual diagnosis—for instance, a client has problems with the temporal lobes, but also has ADD or depression—we always treat the temporal lobes first, and then in a few weeks can add another medication or supplement to rebalance other parts of the brain. (See Dr. Daniel Amen's book, *Healing ADD*, and read the chapter on Type 4: Temporal Lobe ADD.)

3. Try supplements.

Here is a list of some of the supplements that have been used to increase the functioning of the temporal lobes. Fish oil alone has shown great promise in helping a variety of mood disorders including bipolar disorder. Each of the following supplements works differently for different temporal lobe issues and, therefore, should not be used without the advice and direction of a

qualified health practitioner. Temporal lobe issues are perhaps the most delicate and complicated, calling for a professional's guidance.

- GABA
- Valerian
- omega-3 fish oil, sometimes in very high doses, up to 10,000
  grams a day in the case of severe problems, prescribed under the
  care of a physician. (Complications could occur if you are on any
  sort of blood thinner, so please only take high doses of fish oil
  under a doctor's care.)
- Alpha lipoic acid
- Vitamin A and vitamin C as antioxidants
- Phosphatidylserine
- Ginkgo biloba
- Low-dose ibuprofen

4. *Avoid sugar.*

Sugar, we've found, often leads to low blood sugar and then to aggressiveness. Avoiding sugar, corn syrup, alcohol, or high carbohydrates from refined
white flour is especially helpful in balancing temporal lobe mood problems.

5. *Try music therapy.*

The field of music therapy is fascinating and has proven helpful to all ages
and a wide variety of emotional and physical problems. Singing or humming
is excellent for temporal lobe health. "Toning," which is holding a note like
"ah" or "mmmm," as in the classical Gregorian chants, has shown to calm the
brain. Listening to classical music seems to delight even babies in utero and has
not only a calming effect on humans, but also seems to make us able to learn
information more easily. Finally, playing a musical instrument is yet another
way to nourish your brain. I have noticed that my clients who struggle with
their temporal lobes seem to have a stronger than usual affection for music and
often feel they need music the way some people need food, air, and water.

A recent and amazing phenomenon in both the music world and the
world of science is the soaring success of a CD called *Chant* by a group of

Austrian monks who sing ancient Gregorian chants. It actually became the number-one selling disc in classical music and number nine in the pop music category. The music gained huge popularity when paired with the popular video game Halo, but there are other reasons for its continued success. Though beautiful to listen to on its own merit, *Chant* is also being promoted for its health benefits, which some say are substantial.

Dr. Alan Watkins, a senior lecturer in neuroscience at Imperial College London, says that "the musical structure of chanting can have a significant and positive physiological impact" and that chanting has been shown to lower blood pressure, increase levels of the performance hormone DHEA, and reduce anxiety and depression.[4]

There's no doubt that sound has genuine neurological effects, and some studies suggest that music can stimulate the production of endorphins (natural opiates secreted by the hypothalamus) in the brain, help the left and right hemispheres of the brain communicate more effectively (apparently stimulating the immune system), and create new neural pathways in the brain.

"One person who has no doubt about the health benefits of Gregorian chant is Benedictine Sister Ruth Stanley. She is the head of the complementary medicine program at the Central Minnesota Heart Center at St. Cloud Hospital and has had great success easing chronic pain and other ailments by having her patients listen to chant. 'The body can move into a deeper level of its own inherent, innate healing ability when you play chant,' she says. 'About 85 percent of the time, the body goes into very deep healing modes. It's quite remarkable.'"[5]

6. Dance the blues away.

Body movement such as dancing or exercising to music is also good for the brain. For those with temporal lobe issues, combining your exercise routine with music will give you an opportunity to improve your body, brain health, and your mood all at the same time.

One of my close friends fell in love with a man she met at a dance class sponsored by her singles group at church. I encourage everyone I know who is considering marriage to get SPECT scans for herself and her fiancé (and take the Amen brain tests, if possible) as part of premarital counseling. I prefer the SPECT scan over the brain test when it comes to two people who are about to say wedding vows because people can lie or downplay brain issues on the written test to make themselves seem healthier than they may actually be. Not so with the brain scan. Plus, starting their marriage with two balanced brains gives the newlyweds the best possible chance at lasting love.

My friend was so high on love that she forgot that bit of wisdom. She called me in tears when, three years into the marriage, she was not able to take his anger. I asked, "When was the last time you two have gone dancing?" She replied that it had been more than a year. I suggested, "Why don't you go dancing together again and get those good feelings flowing. Then during the dance, say, 'Honey, I love you and I love times like this. I know you don't ever intentionally want to hurt me with your temper. Would you be willing to get a SPECT scan so we can find out if there's anything organic that is causing you to feel so agitated? I want to feel like this with you always and never be frightened of your anger anymore.'"

She did it, and he readily agreed to her suggestion because, with the combination of the movement and music, he could feel and remember the days when love ruled their relationship, before anger arrived to eat away at their love. In this calmed state of mind, he "got it"—and soon, got the "scan and a plan" that helped him bring his best brain to his marriage every single day.

7. Get enough sleep.

Sleep is vital for all brain types, but it is particularly restorative to the sensitive temporal lobes. If you are not getting a good seven to nine hours of deep, restful sleep, your brain is not having a chance to "reboot" its computer, and you will feel on overload. When you sleep, your brain processes and files memories and does a clean sweep of the cobwebs in your head. (Okay, not a very scientific explanation, but you get the gist.) Check with your health practitioner about the possibilities of using natural sleep aid formulas that have GABA, magnesium, melatonin, or a combination of them to help you get to sleep and stay asleep.

Couples often don't realize how a good, restorative night's sleep for both of them can help their marriage improve. If one is snoring or the other is tossing and turning, one or both aren't getting the sleep they need to bring their best brain to the table. Something as simple as a good mattress, some white noise, or dark shades can help a couple sleep well so they can play well together later.

An interesting tidbit: research from the HeartMath Institute shows that when couples fall off to sleep together, after about fifteen or twenty minutes, their heart rhythms are in sync.[6]

8. Consider biofeedback.

Biofeedback clinics have gained popularity as physicians have urged us to find ways to manage our stress. Now, biofeedback is literally in the palm of your hand. One such device is put out by the HeartMath Institute and is called the *emWave* personal stress reliever (see www.emwave.com). The award-winning device is gathering lots of kudos from people who are learning how to manage their own stress with the help of this little handheld device. The Amen Clinic can actually pinpoint certain areas of the brain that need help using specific biofeedback techniques and show on SPECT scans how we can improve our brains through noninvasive biofeedback techniques. It is an exciting area of healing, with no side effects.

9. Take anger management classes.

There are some valuable techniques that can be taught, learned, and practiced to help control tendencies toward explosive anger. I hesitate to recommend anger management classes until I am sure that a person's temporal lobes have been calmed by other means—because the classes don't do a lot of good if your brain is not balanced first. However, the classes and books on anger management are wonderful supplements to the above recommendations in retraining bad habits to more peaceful and productive ways of communicating. Simply Google "anger management classes" in your area or check for related books or classes-on-tape on amazon.com or at your local library.

10. Celebrate good memories.

Because it can be difficult for someone with temporal lobe problems to recall the good times, it is important to emphasize and celebrate all the happy moments in your life. Take pictures, use special plates on special occasions, create a Facebook album of a wonderful memory, and write thank-you notes. Then at the end of each day, jot down one good thing that happened. Maybe you just tried a new flavor of ice cream, and it tasted delicious. Note it, appreciate it, and thank the good Lord for it. This habit will teach your subconscious to ruminate over something positive, even as you sleep, rather than automatically kicking into a negative thought pattern.

TEN TIPS TO HELP AN AGITATED LOVER CALM DOWN

1. Encourage a brain scan.

If your mate shows tendencies of being volatile and you suspect a possible recent or long-ago brain injury, encourage him or her to read this chapter. Or share one of the stories. Let your mate know that you think he is good at heart, but is struggling with a very fixable problem and that you'll do all you can to support his getting help.

2. Catch her being good.

Encourage your mate when she handles a tough situation with calmness or clarity. Compliment her for all the good you see in her heart. Often what we compliment will expand . . . and your mate will enjoy the praise for using self-control and patience.

Remind your mate that she has a good heart even though she is struggling with anger or a temper. See the best in her as often as you can, and let her know you are on her team. You won't take abuse. You need a zero tolerance policy for that. But at the same time, let her know that you understand she is fighting a tough battle in her brain and you are there to support her efforts to get balanced.

3. Notice what calms him.

One woman noticed that her husband was always a calmer, happier version of himself when they went camping as a family. "Something about the out-of-doors just soothes my man's brain. So I adopted the idea that we will do as much as we can outside this year. If the weather is decent, we eat dinner on the back porch or pack a picnic and go fishing. We play Frisbee, golf, or take walks rather than watch TV or play indoor board games. We are even going to a Cowboy Church now—which is held outside in a rodeo arena."

4. *Make music a part of your marriage.*

Join a choir together or take a dance class. Play beautiful music in your home or car that you know soothes the soul. Invest in quality equipment and recordings as part of your mental health, or go to concerts that you both enjoy, or even participate in karaoke nights. If you enjoy playing an instrument or two, have a good old-fashioned sing-along. What happened to those evenings around the family piano or with somebody strumming a guitar on the porch?

5. *Create a sleep haven.*

Do all you can to help create a restful bedroom so your mate can get a good night's sleep. Put bottles of water and any sleep aids or supplements needed, along with some reading material, on the nightstand. Use a fan or a white-noise machine if that helps. Invest in some good shades or drapes. Think of ways you can turn your own bedroom into a luxury spa. Take turns giving each other a massage while playing restful music. Say a short bedtime prayer together for peaceful sleep. Kiss each other good night. As much as it's possible to do so, create a calm space for your partner and for yourself.

6. *Eat balanced meals together.*

If your spouse is willing, try to avoid sugar for a month and see if it doesn't improve the mood in the household. If you are a good cook, get creative with healthy and tasty recipes that are low in sugars. Keep salted roasted almonds or walnuts as snacks, or serve special cheeses with fresh berries.

7. *De-stress yourself.*

If you live with someone who is prone to anger, you need to pamper yourself with whatever calms and refills your soul. Take a slow-movement, yogalike exercise class. Walk out in nature or at the gym a few times a week. Get a massage. Window-shop. Play with your grandkids. Go to lunch with a friend. Meander through a favorite bookstore. Play a sport at the Y. Take an art class, or join a support group or Bible study. Invest in your own peace of mind.

8. *Guard your heart.*

If your spouse has been either verbally or physically abusive, and has been this way for a long time, you may not realize the toll it has taken on your own brain health. People who live with mates who are aggressive and angry tend to suffer from depression, fear, and anxiety—or eventually numb out to life. I would suggest that you step back and take a compassionate look at the effect of living with a volatile spouse. If your mate refuses to get help or treatment, begin to start caring for your own mental health. Books such as *Boundaries in Marriage* by Henry Cloud and John Townsend and *Stop Walking on Eggshells* by Paul T. Mason and Randi Kreger are good places to start recognizing abuse—even "mild" abuse—with suggestions on how to protect yourself and your heart.

9. *Watch out for toxic religion.*

Be aware of the difference between normal enthusiasm for connection to God in worship and toxic religion or religious obsession in your mate. The apostle Paul talked of people who had a "form of godliness" but it was without real power to change lives.

Here are a few warning signs:

- They view God as a cold, harsh, distant taskmaster rather than an approachable, loving Father.
- They are caught up in formulas and rituals that have a compulsive quality to them.
- They are joyless, cynical, and hypercritical.
- They tend to be prideful and isolate themselves more and more from others.
- They are not flexible, are unwilling to change or look within. They persecute those who disagree with their self-righteous views. In other words, they justify their anger as righteous.
- The men in toxic religious environments tend to love and repeat Bible verses (out of context) about women submitting to men. Women: notice a big red flag if your boyfriend or husband is especially enamored by religions or denominations that preach male domination and control or total, mindless submission.

If your mate is showing signs of possible religious compulsions, either get him or her to some professional help (a certified counselor) or, if you meet with resistance, seek some sane, balanced professional support for yourself. It can be easy to feel as though your head is in a blender when living with someone who is toxically religious—and you will need a good, well-qualified Christian counselor as a sounding board to help you navigate through what is normal and what is not.

10. Protect yourself and your children.

You need to have a safe place to go and a safe way to get there should your spouse become violent—verbally or physically. So when things are calm, create a safety plan: put an extra set of keys and some money, along with any phone numbers you may need, where you can get them in an emergency. Abusers will often take and hide your purse, keys, or wallet to keep you stuck. Abuse tends to worsen and amplify with each episode. Because those with temporal lobe issues will often explode and then feel better, they may be contrite for a short time. But if you overlook abuse, it *will* get worse the next time.

Important: I genuinely believe that most verbal and physical abuse is the result of unstable temporal lobes. If there is injury or instability to this area of the brain, the question is not if *abuse will occur; it is a matter of* when. *If you have tried counseling, spiritual warfare, and numerous other interventions, and the rage persists, most likely your mate has a medical problem.*

That said, until the raging spouse is calm enough to submit to some help, you've got to take cover. Abuse must be nipped in the bud, and the only way I have seen this work is by removing yourself and your children from the abuser. Or have legal authorities remove the abuser from you by either calling the police or having a restraining order served. In emergencies, there are women's shelters in nearly every town, and most of them are excellent resources for help. In addition to offering shelter, many of them provide free counseling and other resources for help.

Many women have been hesitant to call the police when their husbands are threatening or abusive, but nothing will get the attention of an abuser and get him help like the wake-up call of a night in jail. Generally the judge will order your mate to take anger management classes and perhaps get a psychiatric evaluation. The legal system will work with you to get restraining orders that can be gradually and safely removed as your husband improves. There are places where supervised visits can take place until the family is safe to operate alone again. It is always better to call for help sooner rather than later if your mate shows tendencies toward abuse or violence. The sooner you get help, the greater the chances are of turning your mate around before it is too late—for him, for you, and for your children.

Many men are hesitant to call for help when their wives are abusive because most men can defend themselves physically, and it is embarrassing to say, "My wife is violently abusive to me." However, if there are children in the home and a wife flies off the handle, the children are sure to suffer. So men: love your wife enough—and love yourself and your kids enough—to seek help. Get strong emotionally, and be firm about her need to have a good evaluation of her brain-mood and possibly of her hormones. If you have to force a crisis to get her to allow you to help her find help, do so. This may mean removing yourself and your children from the home until she agrees to be seen by a qualified doctor familiar with temporal lobe issues. Shore yourself up by seeing a good therapist to help you through this minefield. You'll need all the support you can get.

Please rate yourself on each of the symptoms listed below, using the following scale:

0=Never 1=Rarely 2=Occasionally 3=Frequently 4=Very Frequently N/A=Not Applicable/Not Known

(You answer in one column, your mate in the other column.)

_____ _____ 1. Frequent feelings of nervousness or anxiety

_____ _____ 2. Panic attacks

_____ _____ 3. Heightened muscle tension (headaches, sore muscles, hand tremors)

_____ _____ 4. Periods of heart pounding, rapid heart rate, or chest pain

_____ _____ 5. Periods of trouble breathing or feeling smothered

_____ _____ 6. Periods of feeling dizzy, faint, or unsteady on your feet

_____ _____ 7. Periods of nausea or abdominal upset

_____ _____ 8. Periods of sweating, hot or cold flashes

_____ _____ 9. Tendency to predict the worst

_____ _____ 10. Fear of dying or doing something crazy

_____ _____ 11. Avoidance of places for fear of having an anxiety attack

_____ _____ 12. Avoidance of conflict

_____ _____ 13. Excessive fear of being judged or scrutinized by others

_____ _____ 14. Persistent phobias

_____ _____ 15. Low motivation

_____ _____ 16. Excessive motivation

_____ _____ 17. Tics (motor or vocal)

_____ _____ 18. Poor handwriting

_____ _____ 19. Quick startle

_____ _____ 20. Tendency to freeze in anxiety-provoking situations

_____ _____ 21. Lack of confidence in own abilities

_____ _____ 22. Shyness or timidity

_____ _____ 23. Embarrassment at minor situations

_____ _____ 24. Sensitivity to criticism

_____ _____ 25. Biting fingernails or picking of skin

Results: If there are five or more symptoms that are at a level 3 or 4, then there is a high likelihood that a SPECT scan would show overactivity in the basal ganglia, the area of the brain associated with fear and anxiety.

From Amen Brain Subsystem Checklist, used by permission from Dr. Daniel Amen and the Amen Clinic.

CHAPTER EIGHT

The Anxious Lover (Basal Ganglia)

Ultimately we know deeply that on the other side of every fear is a freedom.
—MARILYN FERGUSON

I n Gene Wilder's audio-memoir, he talked of getting lost driving home from rehearsal in downtown Hollywood, and for some reason he started feeling sick and anxious. Not because he was lost—he'd been lost before—and not because it was a bad neighborhood because it wasn't. He pulled over to the side of the road and looked up and saw that he'd accidentally driven into the area of town where he'd been sent to private school as a young boy—a school where he'd been regularly beaten up by boys who had it in for Jewish kids. What his mind didn't recognize, his body remembered. In fact, we call these episodes or triggers *body memories*.[1]

If you ever smelled a scent or heard a song that put you in a melancholy or anxious frame of mind before your brain registered the connection to a frightening or painful memory, you've experienced body memory. And you've experienced your basal ganglia at work. Here are some differences between people with normal and overactive basal ganglias:

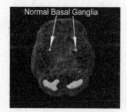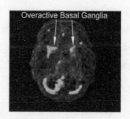

Normal basal ganglia and overactive basal ganglia

Normal	Overactive
Have sense of calm	Are tense, nervous
Have normal muscle movement	Have tremors, tics
Feel pleasure	Have difficulty feeling pleasure
Are able to confront problems	Will avoid conflict
Can manage anxiety under stress	Have headaches, shoulder and neck tension, migraines, colitis, stomach tension; anxious, panicky
Touch is comforting	Touch may be distressing or irritating

I know a woman whose second, happy marriage was experiencing some issues because of lingering bad memories from her first marriage. Without meaning to, sometimes her current husband would say something that triggered an anxiety response in his sensitive wife. Many women have similar experiences after having suffered childhood or teen sexual abuse. They marry good men, but their bodies carry some painful memories that become hard to overcome during lovemaking. I hope this story will encourage you. There is hope and healing for the anxious lover. I'll let Debbie tell her story in her own words. (Names have been changed.)

My mom said that from the time I was young, I had an enormous desire to please. I was also very easily embarrassed, leaning toward being shy. I had a tender heart toward all God's creatures—be they human or animal. Or plastic, as in my baby dolls, which I cared for as tenderly as any five-year-old "mother" could. Also, I was easily overwhelmed and frightened. I used to be terrified of the ten o'clock news and things under my bed. The wicked witch from *The Wizard of Oz* could keep me in nightmares for a month. Like most kids, I feared rejection. I feel pretty sure that I was born with a basal ganglia that operated a little higher than average. (My sister also has battled anxiety, as has my daughter. So I think there is probably a genetic bent toward Chicken Little-itis!) Most of all, I was nice.

As it turned out, too nice, too often, for my own good.

I married too young—at age seventeen—to a confused, lost puppy of a teenage boy who himself was barely eighteen.

Nearly three decades later, I was still married to the same boy-man who had grown older and had fathered our three children but had matured only in years. Mentally, he'd only grown more confused and lost. If anything, he was less mature in his forties than he was in his late teens. (In fact, I remember in a rare moment of truth, he said, "Debbie, I am just not a mature person. You should probably just accept that.")

Like a playground bully, he played games with my tender heart and seemed to get pleasure from the joy of one-upping me or pulling the wool over my eyes. Mostly he longed for a new toy or stimulant to keep him from feeling numb and morose. (These could come in the form of other women to flirt with, rock climbing without a rope, running away for days without telling me where he was, and pot and alcohol binges.) Almost from the moment we said, "I do," it seemed he internally began saying, *Or maybe, I don't.*

The Pollyanna People Pleaser in me longed to become whatever he needed, to do anything but face the unthinkable agony of being unwanted and rejected. Every so often I would feel I had succeeded, that I'd turned his heart toward me—but it was always short-lived. Eventually, inevitably, his nose would be pressed up against the window of our marriage as if the bonds of matrimony were a cage from which he longed to escape. No amount of cooing or preening could coax him into turning his heart toward our home or me for any length of time.

I jumped through so many hoops that I should have won an Olympic medal in trying to please a man. I also got a degree in walking on eggshells around a husband whose temper and likes and dislikes were as unpredictable as the weather. For most of my married life, I would simply wake up and think to myself, *How do I remain sane and calm in this marriage today? How do I stay with a man who doesn't love or want me, for the sake of our children and family? Is there anything else I can say, do, change, or better in myself to make him love me?*

Some days I survived better than others. There were a few times I fought suicidal feelings, the pain was so intense. But mostly my neck stayed in a knot, my stomach was always in upheaval, and a part of my heart stayed on hyper-alert—preparing to be crushed, hurt, confused, played games with, or abandoned at any moment. And because I was so young when we married and so convinced that God hates divorce and, therefore, that would not be an option, I didn't realize how horribly dysfunctional my marriage was. It's amazing how our minds will normalize what is truly unacceptable when we are just trying to survive. Anything to keep the status quo going because the pool of sorrow in our lives seems somehow less frightening than jumping into the Great Unknown. Denial was my very good friend for a very long time.

My lost puppy was eventually diagnosed with narcissistic personality disorder. The best way I know how to describe a person with NPD is that they are people with a black hole within, and they seek others to feed their starving bottomless egos—but are never satiated for long. To try to fill this hole of need, they spend a lot of time searching for "fixes"—and polishing the mirror of an image of themselves that they've constructed. But there is no real sense of self inside. No authentic human being in touch with their true feelings—just a series of fragile images. *Men Who Can't Love* is just one such book written about this type of personality. I now know that many people with NPD also have brain imbalances, and I do wonder if a SPECT scan would have been a life-changer for this melancholy, perpetually unsatisfied soul I married.

When I finally discovered that my husband had been secretly, serially unfaithful over years of our marriage, along with the years I'd endured of being verbally, mentally, and sometimes physically abused, I somehow found the strength to file for divorce even though it meant everything dear and familiar would blow up around me: the family portrait, the family home, ministry. Who was I apart from being a married woman? I'd never been single—never lived alone. The newly divorced woman in the movie *Under the Tuscan Sun* was amazed that divorce doesn't actually kill you. Oh, do I understand that! He would not file for divorce because it would have made him look bad, but as our counselor put it so well, "Neither would he lift a finger to love you or invest even an ounce of effort into your marriage." By the time I stumbled into a lawyer's office (with a dear friend to hold me up), I was fighting for my very emotional existence.

Let's fast-forward from that bad dream into the healthy, amazing, nurturing marriage I enjoy today with my second husband. I often tell people, "I married a grown-up, and—it's glorious!" I am married to a loving man with the desire to protect, care for, and love me rather than trick, abandon, or abuse me. The day I married Gene, it was like walking out of a war zone of survival into a safe, loving, happy world where I could finally, deeply exhale. In fact, every time I hear Louis Armstrong sing "What a Wonderful World," I feel that is the theme song for my life today.

So why then did I sometimes find myself curled up in the fetal position by something benign that Gene—this loving, faithful, adoring husband of mine—had said? Why, when I found myself disagreeing with something during a normal marital discussion, did I long to grab my purse and keys and flee?

Why did I still suffer from nightmares related to being trapped in my previous marriage?

Would I ever be totally free of fear and anxiety from my past so that I could fully live in, embrace, and relish today?

I read one of Dr. Daniel Amen's books and then another and another. I knew from the self-test that I probably had an overactive basal ganglia. Then one day I met Dr. Henslin, and he concurred that this issue was probably very real but more encouraging, very treatable!

"Dr. Henslin," I said, "I know that this good husband of mine deserves a wife with a brain that doesn't punish him for what a sick puppy did to me in the past. I am tired of feeling stuck in a place of anxiety and fear. I want to be healed."

I got a brain scan, and it showed a diamond pattern that involves not only an overactive basal ganglia but also overactivity in the cingulate and limbic system as well. This is most often the pattern of post-traumatic stress disorder (or PTSD). I began taking at night a good supplement with GABA in it along with melatonin, and not only did my nightmares disappear; I slept through the night like a baby.

When I felt anxiety rise during the day, I'd also take my GABA supplement. I used a "tapping technique" (www.emofree.com) and also did what I called "intentional memory overlays" to help heal some of the worst and most persistent bad memories. For example, I would replay a scene in my head where my ex-husband would be saying something devastating, and then I would very vividly imagine my new, kind, and loving husband walking into the room, pulling me into his arms, and saying, "Those things are not true. I love you, and we are getting out of here together." Now I cannot visualize the Bad Scene without imagining the Happy-Ending Scene with it. I've simply reminded my brain of the truth in a visual way—and turned from traumatized victim to healthy, beloved wife.

I've also learned that to stop a traumatic looping thought, I need to do something physical, like walking to the park or engaging in a mentally absorbing task that knocks the gerbil off of the wheel and allows me to redirect my thoughts. Going to a movie is very helpful because a movie touches so many of the senses in a big way that I'm unable to do anything but let my brain get absorbed and caught up in the story. Playing a mind-absorbing game or even doing a crossword puzzle is also helpful. It's my way of shaking that pesky thought out of my head and moving on with life! Sometimes I'll play Carly Simon's "Haven't Got Time for the Pain" to remind me to live in the present moment and that I don't have time to let the past rob me of my happy todays!

My husband is happy to be supportive and knows when I get that deer-in-the-headlights look that I am probably going to need a little more patience and help to get back into reality. He's learned to ask me, "What do you need? How can I help? Want to go to a movie? Take a walk?" He also put many of my fears aside when he told me, gently, "You never have to leave or run away because I am never going to leave you. And you never have to speak to me in anger because I will always listen to whatever you need to say and do everything I can to make things right between us." He somehow sensed my deepest fears and knew how to calm them with this loving reassurance. And he kept his promise. He's never walked out on me, never raised his voice in anger, always listened to me, and done everything he could to help.

Though I may still get tripped up and triggered by something that kidnaps my emotions with an old painful memory, it happens very rarely now, and if it does happen, we have tools to help reorient and reconnect me to the lovely truth of my present life.

FREEDOM IS JUST ANOTHER WORD FOR . . . A CALMED BASAL GANGLIA!

Leanne was referred by her pastor to our office because this delightful woman in her fifties was struggling with severe anxiety and had a secret obsession with her weight. She was soaked in shame. "My being referred to a therapist's office just shows what a spiritual failure I am," she said.

During the initial session she admitted that during her decades-long marriage she had never experienced a single orgasm. I encouraged her to get a SPECT scan after looking at the results of her written Amen brain test. I suspected the basal ganglia was overactive, but wanted to make sure I wasn't missing something else. As I thought, her scan showed that her basal ganglia was way overactive. Her history revealed that anxiety had been a chronic problem since she'd been a preteen.

"Did anything happen to you at that age?" I asked. She acknowledged having had a girlish crush on a camp counselor, who ended up molesting her. Her struggles with anxiety and panic began after the camp and prior to her starting the new school year.

I suggested several blood tests. We found that her blood sugar was unstable, so we tweaked her diet and supplements to keep her blood sugar stable (small snacks or meals throughout the day with some protein each time, reduced sugar and white flour as well). High doses of fish oil (omega-3 fatty acids) also helped nourish the neurotransmitters that would calm her basal ganglia.

A hormone panel revealed that her progesterone levels were also very low, so she began taking progesterone. If she had gone to a general practitioner with her anxiety issues, there is a good chance he would have put her on antianxiety medication. Sadly, most of these medications are not good for the brain, long-term. We can see deteriorations over time, similar to brains on street drugs or alcohol. So when someone has high anxiety, I look at every other system in the body that might be bolstered, rather than suggest medication as a first line of treatment.

In time, her brain calmed down, her muscles relaxed, and in therapy she was able to pour out the pain she'd felt from the sexual abuse. She acknowledged shame at feeling a mixture of some pleasure along with terror during the molestation. I explained to her that her mixed bag of feelings was very common with sexual abuse at a young age by a trusted person.

During the week following the session where she was able to be totally honest about the past abuse, she surprised herself by initiating lovemaking with her husband on two different occasions. Her husband was pleasantly surprised by her newfound sexual interest and desire. Playfulness returned to their marriage. He kiddingly said to her, "Sweetie, if you want to, you can go to therapy sessions twice a week!" She, full of newfound spunk and sexual confidence teased back, "I don't think you can handle it!"

TEN TIPS TO CALM AN ANXIOUS LOVER

1. Recognize you can take back control of your brain.

It is very empowering to clients when I assure them that they can control their anxiety. There are a few techniques that I've found helpful. There's a wonderful classic book, *Feel the Fear and Do It Anyway*, in which the author talks about the miracle of "acting as if."[2]

For example, one lady told me, "I'm afraid of mingling in social situations. Really, I almost panic just thinking about it. So I will often think of Paula Deen, who is this wonderful Southern, open-hearted lady on the Food Network channel. She used to have agoraphobia, and now she's having the time of her life and she's become the life of the party! I think to myself, *What would Paula Deen do? How would she act in a group of people?* She always focuses on the other person and makes them feel loved and comfortable and charming. So I try to do that. It helps!"

Another technique is to add something of comfort, something familiar, to an uncomfortable situation. One friend brings a comfy throw and soothing iPod to the cold dentist office. When I speak in public, I like to have one or two friends in the audience whom I know I can look at and get some encouraging eye contact, smiles, and head nods.

2. Stomp on your ANTS.

Dr. Amen often speaks of automatic negative thoughts, or ANTS. I have found that when people have high anxiety, they really do need to retrain their brains. The Scriptures speak of "taking every thought captive" and of "renewing our mind." One way to do this is to exchange our worries for God's reassurances. Another is to become a bystander to your thoughts—questioning their validity and asking yourself: *Is there another way to think about the same situation that might be more true? More kind? More uplifting and positive?*

Here are some ANT categories that Dr. Amen has found can be a real drain and strain on your brain:

- *Mind reading*: Thinking that you know that another person is thinking something negative about you without her telling you. In all our combined years of counseling others, we still cannot read another person's mind. Neither can you.
- *Fortune-telling*: Predicting a bad outcome to a situation before it has occurred. Your mind makes happen what it sees. Unconsciously, predicting failure will often cause failure. You may assume a person won't like you, and because you've already put up a protective shell, he very well may not like you!
- *Always or never thinking*: This is thinking in words such as *always, never, every time,* or *everyone*. These thoughts are overgeneralizations that can alter behavior. If you assume that your mate or your children will never change or *can* never change, you actually lock

them into a mold from which they cannot escape (at least in your
mind).

- *Guilt beatings*: Being overrun by thoughts of *I should have done . . .
  I'm bad because . . . I must do better at . . . I have to . . .* Guilt is
  powerful at making us feel bad. It is a lousy motivator of behavior.

Another recommendation is to simply talk back to your mind the way a
sassy teen might talk back to an adult. In this case, it is okay! Tell your ANTS
to take a hike, and invite APTS (automatic positive thoughts) in, instead.

3. Focus and melt away tension.

Focus your attention on where the feeling of anxiousness is in your body
and keep your attention there until the feeling moves or dissolves. For
example, the tension could be in your abdomen or your neck. Whenever
your attention wanders, bring it back to the place in your body where the
physical feeling is and imagine a warm, healing light . . . melting away that
tension. Doing this for five or ten minutes can reduce, if not eliminate, the
anxiety. A hot bath may also help facilitate this relaxation.

4. Talk down from the ledges.

For many people, just talking through an issue can be almost instantly
calming and turn a giant fear into a normal problem. If you can't talk to someone, try writing a letter or visiting an appropriate Internet chat room. Or pick
up a book like *This Is Your Brain on Joy* or *Feel the Fear and Do It Anyway.*

One client told me, "Talking to my mother, who is very controlling and
often disapproving, is always stressful. So I have a friend I call before talking
to my mother who reminds me that I am a grown-up, I can love my mom
without taking on her guilt, and goes over all the things I've learned in
therapy. Sometimes I have to call my friend to debrief from my mom after-
ward. I return the favor for her when she has to talk to her bossy father!"

Talk to God in conversational prayer, because he is always online, always
listening. *The Message* interprets Philippians 4:6–7 like this:

Don't fret or worry. Instead of worrying, pray. Let petitions and
praises shape your worries into prayers, letting God know your

concerns. Before you know it, a sense of God's wholeness, everything coming together for good, will come and settle you down. It's wonderful what happens when Christ displaces worry at the center of your life.

These are a great couple of verses to write on a card and place where you can see and memorize them when you feel anxious thoughts coming on.

Devotionals such as *Jesus Calling* by Sarah Young and the classic *God Calling* by A. J. Russell can be very helpful in training your brain to hear the kind and comforting voice of God. And other books can be like good friends when you need them. I highly recommend two books by Joan Webb, recovering perfectionist and life coach: *The Relief of Imperfection* and *It's a Wonderful Imperfect Life: Daily Encouragement for Women Who Strive Too Hard to Make It Just Right.*

5. Exercise anxiety away.

In the excellent book *Spark*, Dr. John R. Ratey extols the research-based benefits of exercise on a wide variety of mood issues. He tells the story of a client named Amy, who struggled with anxiety but found that medication left her feeling too lethargic. Yoga was calming, but it turned out that aerobic exercise was her answer. She learned that if she became anxious or panicky at home, she could step onto her elliptical trainer for a few minutes and quell the feelings on the spot.

She uses exercise the way someone might take a shot of liquor or a Xanax—but this solution doesn't leave her hung over or dopey. Some anxious-prone patients prefer slow movement exercise; some find aerobic conditioning is the key. Try both and see what works best for you.

6. Remix your negative scenes (tapping and EMDR as well).

Take a little time to rewrite the anxiety-producing scenes or speeches that loop around in your brain. Question your thoughts. Recognize that others have learned to respond differently to the same set of circumstances—so can you. Become the director in the movie of your life. Know when to yell, "Cut!" on the scene in your head and direct a different ending.

For example, if you are anxious about serving dinner to guests, ask yourself why and how you can take the stress out of the thought process. Do you think everything has to be perfect? Do you *have* to make a gourmet dinner? Remind yourself of a fun evening you enjoyed at someone else's house because the hostess had fun and not because the dinner was perfect. Maybe you can just order pizza, whip up a simple salad, and buy some of your bakery's special dessert. Make life easy and enjoy your friends. Relax.

Also, check out tapping or EMDR practitioners in your area. The wonderful thing about these techniques is how quickly they work, so the investment of money and time for one or two sessions may be all you need.

7. Join the I-refuse-to-soak-in-bad-news club.

Limit listening to or reading the news since it is basically all the bad news in the world boiled down into a depressing and anxiety-producing thirty-minute slot. There's a saying in the newsrooms of the world: "If it bleeds, it leads." The sole reason for whether or not to air a story may be whether it is shocking, gruesome, or anxiety-producing enough to grab an audience's attention. It has nothing to do with the 90 percent of wonderful things happening in the real world. When you watch too much TV, especially downer shows, it can begin to distort the world into an almost totally negative mold. Sadly, the healing, the love, the peaceful efforts, the beauty around the world that happens every single day remains mostly unaired on TV. We have to remind ourselves that the ten o'clock news is *not* the real world. It's the worst and most narrow slice of the evil in the world. Recent studies have shown that depression rates go up with the amount of TV watched beyond a couple of hours a day.

8. Use calming nutrition and supplements.

Follow the Joy Diet in Appendix A. Then know that if you are feeling especially anxious you'll want to have a meal or snack that has some calming, nutritious carbs. A banana cut in half lengthwise and smeared with peanut butter, a bowl of cereal with blueberries, yogurt with fruit, a bowl of oatmeal or Malt-O-Meal, pasta or macaroni and cheese, or a bowl of mashed potatoes with a sprinkle of cheese or meat are all soothing and calming to wound-up minds. One couple has a nightly bag of "bedtime" popcorn (light on the butter) and swears it works better than a sleeping pill to make them chill out and get drowsy.

A glass of wine at a happy hour or with your dinner is calming to many people; however, it can also cause heartburn or middle-of-the-night insomnia for some. Alcohol tends to make people feel relaxed at first but can actually produce more anxiety or irritability with the passage of a little more time. It is also a depressant and should be avoided by people who are already feeling low. Chamomile tea with a little cream and honey is probably a better choice for most.

Supplements recommended:

- Kava, 5-HTP, or St. John's wort are all good for anxiety.
- GABA, or better yet, a combination formula with the amino acid GABA such as Gaba Calm, True Calm, or Dr. Amen's product, NeuroGABA. Follow the directions on the bottle or from your trusted health practitioner.
- 300 mg magnesium can be very relaxing before bed and helps many people with migraines (don't take on an empty stomach). If this amount causes loose bowels, cut back some. Most people find this amount is actually very helpful to their digestive systems.
- You may also try melatonin, a hormone that helps us sleep, which is abundant in children but begins decreasing steadily after puberty until there is 90 percent less of it in our bodies by age 70. *(A warning: A very safe supplement, melatonin has been known to increase libido, but it also may decrease libido or ability to orgasm in some people. Just note your sexual responses if you try melatonin as a sleep aid. In fact, many supplements, vitamins, and over-the-counter drugs can affect your sexual feelings positively or negatively. This is a good reason to add just one supplement at a time, and give it a week to note any adverse symptoms: breast tenderness, difficulty in reaching orgasm, slowed libido, irritability, or ultrasensitivity are common signs that something you are taking may be affecting the delicate hormone balance within.)*

9. *Take medication.*

Though antianxiety drugs like Xanax are often prescribed for fearful tendencies or PTSD, I am hesitant to suggest them except in the most severe cases and only for the short term. (It's probably no surprise that Xanax is one of the favored drugs that is prescribed by doctors and then resold among teens and college-age students.) It has a similar effect on the brain that some street drugs have, and after viewing SPECT scans of brains on some of the stronger antianxiety meds, we know they are not good for long-term brain health. Plus, they have an addictive side to them, so we don't encourage their use except for short periods of time and if there isn't an alternative that will work better.

Note: The following chart contains Dr. Daniel Amen's general recommendations to physicians. It is for general information only and not a substitute for your doctor's protocol. However, you may want to share this chapter and the following information with your physician if you or a loved one is having anxiety issues. It is for this reason that I am including Dr. Amen's usual dosages. I'd rather err on the side of giving you information that you may not use if you or your loved one is suffering from anxiety than to leave you groping in the dark for a generic guideline. I know I am personally grateful when books are as specific as possible and when doctors are generous with what they have found to be successful for them and their patients. Dr. Amen is one of those generous physicians, for which so many clients and professional colleagues are grateful.

Medication	Dosage
Neurontin	Generic name for this medication is gabapentin. Preferred medication if no symptoms of manic or bipolar are present. Begin at lowest dose possible, usually 100 mg 3 times a day. Have had patients who have had to start at 50 mg 3 times a day, taking a capsule and using half of it.
Gabitril	Highly effective for anxiety. Start with 2 mg tablets. Take ½ to 1 tablet nightly for 3 to 5 days, then increase to ½ to 1 tablet 2 times daily. Gradually increase until symptom management is reached.
Topamax	Starting dose usually 25 mg at night, and after 3 to 5 days, morning dose is added. Can be increased 25 mg at a time to a max of 100 mg twice daily. For some people, there is a side effect of weight loss. Seems to help with sugar cravings. There are increasing numbers of research articles that point toward the use of Topamax with eating disorders. Watch for memory impairment.

Xanax	Xanax is often prescribed for panic attacks. If a person is a recovering alcoholic, or there is alcoholism in your family background, attempt to use Xanax on a short-term basis, since there is a risk of addiction. Many times Xanax, Klonopin, or Ativan are given with Prozac, Lexapro, Effexor, or Cymbalta. These medications for some people can increase basal ganglia activity while helping with depression. Many times Xanax can be reduced or eliminated if Neurontin or Gabitril is used to help calm basal ganglia overactivity. If Xanax is used on a long-term basis, it can with some people have a side effect of depression and memory problems. Make sure any elderly people in your life are carefully evaluated if using Xanax on a routine basis.
Xyrexa and Resperidal	Xyrexa and Resperidal are sometimes given to help with panic and anxiety in small doses. These medications will often be used if a person is going through a bout of insomnia. These medications are part of a class called "novel antipsychotics" and are also helpful with people who struggle with bipolar or schizophrenia. In small doses it can help with panic or sleep. It works as a dopamine inhibitor. If you use it to sleep and find it is a struggle to get going in the morning . . . or your brain does not "wake up" until 10 or 11 a.m., it can be the Xyrexa or Resperidal causing that to happen. We need dopamine in the frontal cortex in the morning to feel motivated to even get out of bed. If you are having trouble "waking up," tell your prescribing MD or your therapist. No need to lose a job or be unable to drive to work safely or drive the kids if your brain is not online.

10. Try aroma and water therapy.

Take a bath with essential oils of lavender, orange, marjoram, and/or chamomile dispersed in the water. Epsom salts allow magnesium to be absorbed through your skin and will relax your muscles and mind.

TEN TIPS TO SOOTHE YOUR ANXIOUS MATE

1. Consider a pet.

Stroking a pet with soft fur (and/or a purr) has been shown to reduce anxiety. If you are up to the mess and care and feeding of a pet, you may consider adopting one. Be sure to choose a calm breed of animal.

2. Massage your mate.

One of the best gifts you could possibly give your spouse is to either take a class or read a book or watch a video on how to give a relaxing massage. Take a hot bath or shower together, put on some soft music, then warm some massage lotion or oil and indulge your mate with a relaxing treat of touch. Learn what sort of touch most calms your man or woman. A quick foot or back rub is a quick way to massage away stress for many couples. One happy couple in their seventies told me, "We bought a little lotion warmer and keep it in the living room. While watching TV, we give each other a foot rub before bed. At our age, this is almost better than sex!"

(Look for lotion warming dispensers online. Conair makes one. Most will heat up in two minutes and keep the lotion warm for up to an hour. A nice little luxury gift for Valentine's Day, your spouse's birthday, or Christmas.)

3. Get busy doing something distracting.

Doing anything physical—taking a walk or digging in a garden together—can stop the loop of fearful thoughts. Offer to take your mate to a movie or go for a walk or window-shop. Maybe get out a jigsaw puzzle or a Scrabble game. Note what absorbs his mind and gets him away from the worry-loop, and help him redirect his thoughts with a little bit of action.

4. Hug her tight.

When your mate is feeling especially anxious, just pulling her into your arms for a good, long hug can be very comforting. Or lie down on the bed or couch for a full-bodied hug—head to toe. Your wife will often calm considerably if you just let her lie in your arms, her head on your chest, and stroke her hair or back.

5. Enjoy hot water therapy together!

Couples who shower or bathe together tend to be happier, and no wonder! Hot water or a bubble bath puts us in a state of deep relaxation, and when we do it together, it is especially bonding. One of my couple friends, a very happy couple I might add, tell me they have regular "bathtime board meetings"—meaning they'll fill up their big double tub with relaxing bubbles, bring a glass of wine or cup of hot tea, and catch up on the news of the day in warm-water bliss. Adding lavender oil and Epsom salt can upsize the relaxation just that much more.

6. Offer a cup of hot tea.

There are many herbal teas on the market that have calming properties. Celestial Seasons has their Tension Tamer. Chamomile and decaf Earl Grey both have relaxing properties. Green tea contains l-theanine, an amino acid that is known for reducing anxiety. Keep a kettle on your stove and honey or agave nectar or stevia nearby. Regularly offer your anxious lover a "spot of tea." The warmth of the cup, the calming ingredients, and your loving-kindness will calm his furrowed brow.

7. Create a safe and positive home.

You have the ability to help create the "vibes" in your own home that aid and comfort a mate with high anxiety. Think about the way health spas use all the senses to create a place that makes you say, "Ahhh . . ." when you walk into their space. How many of their relaxation tricks can you use in your home?

Soft lighting: Dimmer switches or lamps can create a soft and soothing light. Candles or the new artificial candles that operate on batteries can also create real ambience. And there's nothing like a fire in the hearth in winter to calm an anxious soul.

Fish: A fish tank or even a couple of goldfish in a fancy bowl are soothing to watch.

Scents: Spas use scents like lavender and eucalyptus to create a feeling of energy and health.

Citrus water: Many spas serve chilled water with slices of lemon and orange to refresh on a hot day, or warm teas on a chilly day.

Music: The music is usually instrumental—soft and soothing. Or sometimes you'll hear the sounds of nature—rain, wind, and ocean.

Touch: Everything is soft and comfortable and pleasant to the skin—soft robes, cool sheets, and comforting blankets.

Color: Most spas use soft whites or creams, tans or browns, and some variation of blue-green in their color scheme. There is a reason for this: the colors of the sea and sand are some of the most relaxing on earth.

Calming voices: Notice the tone of your voice; is it calming, soothing, reassuring, and pleasant?

8. Reassure and reassure.

You can probably never say enough reassuring words, compliments, or loving phrases to your mate. Most anxious lovers are afraid, at a deep level, that they are not meeting up to expectations or desires. Reassure your spouse of your love, notice and compliment him daily, give him plenty of affection, and let him know he is safe to "exhale" with you. Many anxious lovers have the "love language" of verbal affirmation and touch. Make sure you are giving your spouse love in the way he most feels and needs it.

9. Take mini-vacations and getaways.

If your husband or wife has had a particularly tough week, consider getting a hotel room (even if it is in town) for a night. Plan a day trip away from anxiety. Choose a trip that would be most relaxing—whether that means a hike in the country or a half day at a hotel spa. Some areas have hot springs where you can relax in a mineral pool outdoors.

10. Make love.

Lovemaking can be a real anxiety reducer for many. So if you and your spouse are so inclined, jump into bed and get that oxytocin flowing! If your lover is anxious about his desirability or ability to perform—take all the pressure off of him. Tell him how much you love his body, how attracted you are to his heart, and say, "Let's just get naked and snuggle. No expectations! Whatever happens, happens; whatever doesn't—no biggie."

CHAPTER NINE

The Secret to Lasting Love

In the book *Jacob the Baker* by Noah ben Shea, there's a wonderful line: "Jacob was a reed, and the breath of God blew through him, made music of him."

Ultimately this is where we are headed. The goal of this book is not just to give you "love tools," but to help you become a living instrument through which God's love can flow freely, so you can make beautiful music together. To truly be God's love, in human form, to the one you vowed to love for all time, you'll need more than a balanced brain and more than a great sex life; you'll need all of heaven's help you can get. You need the Holy Spirit filling you, renewing you, reminding you to love your mate as Jesus would.

There's a phrase I am hearing more and more these days in theological conversation. It's that we need to be more "incarnational beings" in this world. What in the world does that mean? It means that in the same way Jesus became like us in order to show what God was really like, we are to become God-with-skin-on (by being vessels of his love) to each other. A tall order. Actually, an impossible one. But "with God all things are possible" (Matt. 19:26). And with his help, we can become mirrors of God's love to our mates.

When your husband looks in your eyes, does he see how Jesus would look at him? When your wife asks you a question, do you answer her with the same love and respect that Jesus showed to women?

Using the lessons so far in this book, you've discovered the importance of bringing your best brain to the marriage. This is like a good, solid car for the two of you to drive. You've learned that regular touching and lovemaking, naturally mingled with a healthy spiritual life, is vital. This is the gas in the tank of your marriage.

Now that you have a good car and a full tank of gas—now that you are able to speak the language of love fluently, maturely, and from your highest and most centered selves—I'd like to give you the Road Map to Ultimate

Marital Joy. It's an ancient map, which frankly, I've borrowed from the apostle Paul—the most passionate passage in the New Testament, his letter to the church of Corinth. First Corinthians 13 is often called the "Love Chapter" and I'll bet at least half of you heard your pastor read portions of it at your marriage ceremony. (If you weren't too queasy from nerves and excitement to hear anything anyone said.)

I'd like to look at Paul's map to love from the view of theology and neurology.

TWUUU WUV

If you've ever seen the movie *The Princess Bride*, it can't escape your attention that the theme of the movie is the power of true love, or as the hilariously tongue-tied priest calls it, "twuuu wuv."

From the beginning of time, philosophers, seekers, and romantics have sought to define love, the real thing. But none has managed to encapsulate its essence as well the apostle Paul in the thirteenth chapter of 1 Corinthians. And if ever there was a motley crew in need of some basic instruction in love, it was the wild and woolly Corinthians who might have made up the most dysfunctional church in the Roman world. From fighting over who got the biggest piece of bread and biggest glass of wine at the Lord's Supper, to sleeping with their relatives, to trying to outtalk and one-up each other during church services—the church at Corinth was not exactly the ideal picture of relational maturity.

I love the fresh spin that Eugene Peterson, who interpreted the Bible in modern prose, puts on the introduction to this familiar passage in *The Message*:

The Way of Love
If I speak with human eloquence and angelic ecstasy but don't love, I'm nothing but the creaking of a rusty gate. If I speak God's Word with power, revealing all his mysteries and making everything plain as day, and if I have faith that says to a mountain, "Jump," and it jumps, but I don't love, I'm nothing. If I give everything I own to the poor and even go to the stake to be burned as a martyr, but I don't

love, I've gotten nowhere. So, no matter what I say, what I believe, and what I do, I'm bankrupt without love.

> Love never gives up.
> Love cares more for others than for self.
> Love doesn't want what it doesn't have.
> Love doesn't strut,
> Doesn't have a swelled head,
> Doesn't force itself on others,
> Isn't always "me first,"
> Doesn't fly off the handle,
> Doesn't keep score of the sins of others,
> Doesn't revel when others grovel,
> Takes pleasure in the flowering of truth,
> Puts up with anything,
> Trusts God always,
> Always looks for the best,
> Never looks back,
> But keeps going to the end. (vv. 1–7)

Can't you just feel Paul's passion, energy, and urgency as he penned this passage? I love the truth that without love we are "bankrupt" of heart. As I write this we're in a worldwide recession, and bankruptcy is now as common in California, where I live, as wineries, orange groves, and facelifts. But worse than the lack of funds to pay mortgages are the impoverished hearts of so many "beautiful people" who occupy this land of swimming pools and movie stars. I've never seen so many who look so fit and gorgeous on the outside but feel so bereft of love on the inside.

Paul's Map to Marital Joy provides vital direction for a nation of lovers who've lost their way to relational bliss.

I've grouped and nutshelled Paul's recommendations above into four main categories. I'd like to invite you and your love to take a week and read each of these four sections together. Or perhaps you'd like to read through them all at once, and then spend one week rereading and applying each attribute to your marriage relationship. Think of it as a road trip to becoming relational geniuses.

KINDNESS

I've found, like most of the qualities of love, you really can't give away what you don't give to yourself—or allow God to give to you. It is ultimately God's kindness that woos us to him. Especially poignant are the times when we know we've basically shaken our fists at God by our thoughts and actions, and yet . . . and yet . . . he never stops loving us. Never gives up or picks up his toys and goes home. To experience this kindness ourselves, on a regular basis, is to let our souls fill up with fresh spring water—so we've got an over-flow to share with others who are thirsty for a drop of compassion.

What is kindness? Kindness says, "I want you to be happy." Kindness is often associated with tenderheartedness—which means that your heart is not only able to be empathetic to others in pain; it is moved to help or soothe in some way. Your desire is to see others smile.

> *Kind words can be short and easy to speak,*
> *but their echoes are truly endless.*
> —Mother Teresa

When clients struggle with being kind, I usually find it is rooted in a lack of empathy, which is the ability to put yourself in another's shoes or to feel another's pain. Sometimes the inability to be empathetic is a brain problem. For example, it takes a high-functioning prefrontal cortex to con-nect with feelings and to be empathetic. The presidential control center needs to be online and in good operating condition for someone to connect with feelings and to stay focused on another person in a loving manner. To be kind, we need to think things through before we say them, to be able to have those short inner dialogues where we weigh out how the other person might feel before we say or do something that could land us in the dog-house.

Sometimes empathy is a casualty of a painful and critical past. Often empathy is stunted when we have had to "thicken our skin" because of harsh parents or circumstances over a long period of time, and our hearts are no longer as tender as they were originally created to be. Children who were abused or neglected often have the most difficult time giving and receiving kindness as adults, especially if there was no other mentor or helper who modeled compassionate caring.

Perhaps you've seen the movie *Good Will Hunting*. It's a poignant story about a rebellious, cocky, but brilliant tough guy named Will. In the film, Will (played by Matt Damon) has it all going on: a genius IQ, charm, loyal buddies. He's oozing with big-time potential. He knows the right words to say at the right time to cut a pseudo-intellectual smart guy to shreds, lure someone in when he wants to impress, or deliver a stab to the heart with just the right turn of phrase. The only thing he doesn't know how to do is love or be kind in a truly authentic, empathetic way. He was taught early on by a highly abusive foster father to wrap any real emotion in a cocoon of coolness. Kindness was withheld from him at a critical juncture of youthful development.

As the movie progresses, Will meets a girl with a kind heart, who is beginning to fall in love with him. (And he with her, which frightens Will to the core.) Then he meets Sean (played by Robin Williams), a compassionate, if unconventional, therapist, who returns Will's superficial jabs with buckets of authentic kindness and insight.

Will simply has no idea what to do with these two characters who have arrived in his life: a real woman and real man who are bright, witty, and who actually deeply care for him, pouring buckets of kindness upon him. In other words, they are emotionally healthy enough to know what love is and how to express it. Will, who is all thumbs at loving, goes into automatic I'll-hurt them-before-they-hurt-me mode, a conditioning from his painful past. In one scene, a therapy session, Will (almost as a mental and emotional test) delivers a verbal stab to his therapist's heart when he jokes about Sean's late wife, a woman who'd been the love of this kind man's life. Sean is temporarily disoriented, wounded, and angry. But the next time he meets with Will, he is ready. Ready to tell Will—from the depths of his heart—the difference between a *knowledge about* love and *experiencing* love.

Sean, eerily calm, talks about how his young client could probably offer a classic sonnet about love if asked to define the term. Then the therapist begins to speak of a deep and abiding love a man feels for a woman—a love that speaks volumes from just looking into each other's eyes. A love that bypasses hospital rules so a husband can spend every night in a hospital room with his wife who is dying from cancer.

Sean continues in this vein, revealing what love looks like in action in a marriage, and it looks a lot like kindness. It is a husband who asks his wife after a long day with kids and a migraine: "What can I do to ease your pain a little this evening?" It's the wife who, seeing her husband has a faraway look in his eyes after his boss took him down a few notches at work, says, "Did you know that you are my hero for going into that office and facing the lions each day just to help provide a great home for me and the kids?" Or maybe words are not needed, and she simply takes his hand and leads him to a hot bath, a nice massage, and some sexual healing.

Out of the seven components of love, mutual kindness may be the most essential life trait common to the blessed few. Practiced regularly, kindness will change, soften, and tenderize any heart. It will also increase your capacity to love and be loved.

WAYS TO SHOW KINDNESS TO YOUR MATE

1. *Immerse* yourself *in kindness.*

Kindness flows from people who are also kind to themselves. (Most unkind spouses have an inner critic who is unbelievably harsh and hard on themselves.) Paul says in his letter to the Ephesians that husbands should love their wives as they love their own bodies. "He who loves his wife loves himself," he adds (5:28). In fact, a man who doesn't love himself cannot love his wife well. One woman said to me, "My husband loves me the way he loves himself, all right, which is why I am so miserable in our marriage!" I have also seen the reverse situation, where a woman who scorns her own body is unable to be sexually generous with her mate. So don't skip over this point.

Where can you start being kind to yourself? You begin to open up to loving-kindness by emersion, by daily baptizing yourself, head to toe, in the refreshing waters of kindness. Hang out with people who exhibit qualities of kindness, tenderness, and loving compassion. Look for the Seans who can be mentors in your life: Men who are both tough and tender. Men who are real men but unashamed to love deeply. Women who leave you feeling as though you've been hugged and warmed just by being in their presence. Read books by those who place kindness as a top value in their lives. Absorb all you can on the subject until thinking kindly is automatic, like breathing—until kindness is not only a part of your character but also who you are; until it is the word others, particularly your wife and children, will use in your eulogy someday to describe your very essence.

2. Adopt a kind tone of voice.

When you are tempted to berate yourself or your spouse for a mistake, ask yourself, *Would I talk to a dear friend this way?* (Honestly, many people talk to their dogs more kindly than they speak to themselves or their human loved ones.) If not, then ask how you would lovingly talk to a good friend who'd made a mistake. What tone would you use? This is the voice of love. It is the voice that says, "You are human, and therefore fallible. But you are deeply, eternally loved. Glean whatever lesson you can from this error, make amends, then get up and move forward. Let this experience broaden your compassion and expand your capacity for giving kindness to others." Though it sounds trite, it behooves us to learn to be our own best friends so we can be more generous with others.

A brain check here: the temporal lobes play a significant role in how we hear tone of voice. Where there is instability in the temporal lobes, just a slight increase in tone of voice will tend to be interpreted as critical or angry. If you have temporal lobe issues, step back from your feelings and ask yourself if your emotions are correctly interpreting your mate's comments.

Since whatever we think about is usually what comes out of us, sooner or later, if you accustom yourself to thinking benevolent, merciful, and kind thoughts, this is what will naturally spill over when you talk to your mate, your kids, your friends, your coworkers . . . and strangers at the grocery store (even the ones who have twenty-nine items in their cart at the ten-item-limit fast lane).

3. Turn on your "love gaze."

As often as possible, when your spouse looks at you, make sure he sees what he'd see if he were looking at Jesus. Your eyes are the window to your soul, so soften and focus your eyes on each other. Think of the words to that old praise song, "Turn your eyes upon Jesus, look full in his wonderful face," and remember, *you* are to be Jesus with skin on to your groom. He should see Christ's deep love and acceptance and feel eternally cherished when he looks full into your face.

4. Give a cup of cold water in Christ's name.

Jesus spoke of giving others a "cup of cold water" in his name and said that when we did these sorts of random acts of kindness, we were actually being kind to him. We are passing forward what he gave to us.

So when you bring your mate a cup of coffee in bed, or offer to make her a sandwich, or when you ask if you can run to the store and get milk so she doesn't have to get out in the cold . . . you are passing on the kindness of Christ, in significantly small ways, to your mate.

5. Be generous and creative with kind touches.

If your mate's love language is touch, please be *lavish* with giving this gift of marital kindness. Hold her hand when you walk, snuggle when you watch TV, rub his neck when he's driving, brush her cheek with your hand and gently kiss her as she wakes (without always pushing for more), pat his behind when he's heading out the door as a wordless way to say, "Go get 'em, Tiger!"

Touch is a powerful, quick, and wordless way to be especially kind to your spouse. Look for a variety of ways to lavish the love of your life with touch.

Remember to take the risk of touching or making love, even if you do not feel like it. There are many different types of desire. One type is when you are both hot for each other, particularly after a romantic night or special time together. The most common form of desire in long-term marriages, however, is desire found *while* making love. You may not feel like initiating or responding to sexual overtures, but most loving couples find that once they "just say yes," they are soon very happy they did!

Why Being Kind to Your Mate
Is Also Being Kind to Your Brain

You may have heard that that random acts of kindness, both small and large, produce what is called the *helper's high*. It is as though our Creator wired us to operate at the most joyful brain setting when we live thinking more of others and a little less of ourselves. (An old sweet song, "Less of Me," was written and performed by Glen Campbell back in the late 1960s. Oh, come on and humor this old man by checking it out on YouTube for a wonderfully simple reminder to live a little kinder. Great song to teach the kids too.)

Not only does the helper's high give your brain a happy little buzz; it also makes your body healthier, reversing feelings of depression, isolation, and aggression. When therapists can get someone who is down in the dumps to feel compassion and a desire to help someone else, we often see depression levels drop dramatically. Stress levels also get lower even as the immune system gets stronger. Sleep is more peaceful as well. In fact, study after study emerging from the research on happiness has found a strong correlation between the happiness, well-being, and health of people who are kind.

PATIENCE

I grew up on a farm in southern Minnesota. There were many times when I would take a walk down the dusty, graveled driveway at our house and go across the road to drop in on Albert and Ann Scherger (pronounced "sugar," which proved to be the perfect last name for this amazing couple). My earliest memories are from when I was just five or six years old, making that walk across the street.

They had the most welcoming home I've ever known. I just loved going there, and to this day I can picture Ann's smiling face. She always had milk and cookies for her hungry little friend. I would then make my way from the kitchen to go hang out with Albert. I loved Albert. He would always stop what he was doing, focus on me, and then we would just talk. Eventually I grew up, went to college, got married, and had children, but whenever I made the trip to visit my parents back home, I would also walk down the driveway and cross the street to see the Schergers, just as I did as a child. In fact, even as a grown father myself, when I was at my folks' house I would wake up early as if in anticipation of going to see Albert and Ann. Almost every time I remember this or tell someone else about this simple little ritual, tears of happiness well up. That is how powerful the memory of their patient kindness to me over the decades affected my deep limbic system. Even though I must have interrupted their work or their schedule, day after day, year after year, they received me each time as an honored guest.

> *A waiting person is a patient person.*
> *The word* patience *means the willingness*
> *to stay where we are and live the situation*
> *out to the full in the belief that something*
> *hidden there will manifest itself to us.*
> —Henri J. M. Nouwen

On one of the trips back to Minnesota I got up early one summer morning and looked across the road. I could see Albert on his ATV four-wheeler, working his garden—he had to be in his early eighties at the time—and we had a great time catching up with each other. As I was about to leave to go back, he said, "Earl, do you want to stop in and see Ann?" I had thought it was too early in the morning for Ann to be ready for company, but I welcomed the invitation to say hi to my old friend.

As we stepped in the doorway of their old 1920s farmhouse, Albert said to me, "Earl, Ann won't remember your name. Please do not take it personally. That is just the way it is."

I think this phrase, "It's just the way it is," spoken with great affection and understanding, may be the best definition of patience in marriage I've ever heard. Albert loved his wife as she was losing her memory with the tender, matter-of-fact patience of someone who has tended to his mate, as she tended to him, for decades. So she was losing her memory. That is just the way it was. Not too long after that morning, Albert could no longer take care of Ann, and so he placed her in the local nursing home. He then began the daily trips to see her. Patiently, lovingly, he tended as best he could for the love of his life even when she could no longer remember his name. It was just the way Albert was.

Patience is an amazing virtue to cultivate and practice, right alongside the art of kindness, to put your marriage into the top 10 percent of happy couples.

WAYS TO SHOW PATIENCE TO YOUR MATE

1. *Work toward acceptance and say, "It is what it is."*

Impatience is often a symptom of not being able to accept the truth of the moment with grace. But there is an enormous inner relief that comes with simply admitting that in some areas your mate may never change. Yes, he may be as good as they get, at least in some areas. As long as he is not abusing or abandoning you, there's a lot you can simply put up with, get used to. One man says, "Over the decades my wife's tendency to misplace or forget things has actually become less of an irritant and more of an endearment." Just as Albert learned to say, "It's just the way it is" with his wife—accept her memory loss and move on—so most spouses have some areas where, if their spouse isn't going to change, they can simply change their attitude. Can you, perhaps with a sense of humor or empathy, begin to see one or two of your mate's *irritants* as *endearments?*

2. *See the child within the adult.*

One way to help foster patience in marriage is to look at the history, particularly the childhood wounds that may cause your mate to be irritable or obsessive or forgetful. "When my wife was a child, and her volatile parents would fight, she would turn the music on loud and clean her room top to bottom, arranging her stuffed animals in order of smallest to largest, color-coordinating the clothes in her closet," said one husband. "When we disagree or fight or she feels particularly stressed, guess what she does? Turns the music up loud and begins creating order in her environment as a way to deal with the chaotic feelings in her mind. If I think of her as a little nine-year-old girl trying to cope with her parents arguing, I am so much more loving and patient with her method of creating some sort of control."

Ask your mate, "When you were stressed as a child, how did you deal with it?" You may learn something that stretches your compassion and helps you be more patient.

3. *Just breathe and say, "It's not earth-shattering."*

So your wife is still getting dressed and ready to go out for dinner when your reservation is in five minutes. Men, here's my advice. Breathe. Then say, "It's not earth-shattering if we are late." Call to change your reservation time, eat a cracker with peanut butter if you are starving, and turn on ESPN to distract yourself from pacing and fuming.

Women, if your husband is late for the meal you just prepared: Ditto. Breathe. Then say to yourself, *It's not earth-shattering. It's disappointing, but I am not going to ruin our evening together by ranting over his being late and the food getting cold*. One gal who used to fume when this scenario occurred says, "I began asking myself how could I be both kind to myself and to him in this situation? I'll switch gears and enjoy my dinner outside on the patio with some good jazz on the stereo while the food is still fresh and warm. I'll savor every fabulous bite. Then when he gets home, I'll warm up his dinner, sit with him, and enjoy a glass of wine while he eats. He'd rather have a happy wife than dinner fresh off the grill."

4. Don't get even; get creative.

Rather than automatically getting impatient with your mate, get curious instead. Ask yourself, *What creative alternative could I come up with here that would calm my anxiety and show grace to my spouse?* Think of a situation right now where you tend to get impatient with your mate. Then approach that same situation as if you were a life coach, looking for at least one or two alternatives to the normal response of pacing like a caged lion.

"My wife," says Gene, "usually spends the last few minutes of leaving the house for church or an event frantically looking for her purse, her cell phone, her keys, and her coat. So instead of tapping my foot in aggravation while she runs back and forth all over the place gathering these items, I've learned to gather them for her. So when she's dressed and ready to go, I've already found her cell phone and keys and put them in her purse and am standing at the door with her coat and a calm, collected smile on my face. She's so grateful, and that makes me feel like a bit of a hero." That's a perfect example of a man who got creative instead of getting aggravated.

Most people, even children, who learn the fine art of patience, have really learned the fine art of distracting themselves until the waiting is over. Creatively helping your mate is one great way of keeping busy instead of tapping your foot in aggravation.

5. *Remember the golden rule of patience.*

"Be patient to your wife just as you would like her to be patient with you when you need it." When tempted to look down at or lecture your husband for his shortcomings, mistakes, or quirks, take a split second to remember your own shortcomings, mistakes, and quirks. Give your mate the grace you'd love to receive from others if you'd blown it, made a mistake, or weren't at your best.

Why Cultivating Patience Is Good for Your Brain

Perhaps you've heard of the famous marshmallow experiment done in the 1960s. A group of four-year-olds were given a marshmallow and promised another—if, that is, they could wait twenty minutes before eating the first one.

Some children held out, and others caved in to the temptation. The researchers then followed the progress of each child into adolescence and found that the patient marshmallow group turned out to be better adjusted and more dependable and did better on their academic tests.

Another famous test on the virtue of patience was a "gift delay," in which children were shown a nicely wrapped gift but told they must complete a puzzle before opening it. Researchers then calculated a "delay score" based on how long the children could wait before diving in to open the present. When independent examiners interviewed the test subject years later, they found that boys who lacked impulse control were "irritable" and that the girls were "sulky." In contrast, the patient boys were "attentive" and the girls "competent."

Patience is a virtue in marriage that can be nurtured. If patience proves to be a true impossibility for you, there's a good chance you may need a little supplement or even medication to calm you so that you can better wait for what you want. Those with ADD and cingulate issues, for example, tend to be able to show much more patience when their brain health is improved.

FORGIVENESS

Back in the early '80s, Pia Mellody wrote a book called *Facing Codependence*, which helped put the word *boundaries* on the self-help map. I remember being in a seminar with her as she talked about her relationship with her husband and how they kept the slate clean between them. They had a rule: if you had a hurt, anger, or resentment, you had one week to bring it up. Seven days. If you let that anger simmer past that week, you couldn't bring it up. It wasn't allowed. They found that this rule forced them to keep short accounts on everything in the relationship so that bitterness, couched in silence, didn't have a chance to take root and grow.

She told a story about being in Arizona when every once in a while they'd wake up in the morning, open up the door, and see a big bat on the screen door. And so one morning Pat got up before Pia, saw the bat on the screen door, and—having *had* it with flying pests—shot the offender, putting a hole in the door. (Pat is a bit impulsive, leaning toward "wild man" at times.)

Pia was not amused at being woken by a gunshot or at the sight of a dead creature or at the hole in the screen door. So she expressed her displeasure with his bat-elimination method, and though she was angry, she forgave him, and he promised not to do it again.

A week later, she saw him fixing the screen door, and the memory made her angry all over again. In fact, she started to lecture him again on the foolhardiness of his actions, but he just smiled and said, "The one week is up."

*Forgiveness is the name of love practiced among people
who love poorly. The hard truth is that all people love poorly.
We need to forgive and be forgiven every day, every hour increasingly.
That is the great work of love among the fellowship
of the weak that is the human family.*
—Henri J. M. Nouwen

What I like about the story is that it so well demonstrates how we can deal with resentment; then something else happens that triggers the memory of the hurt. And then, before we know it, we are rehashing something that should be over and done.

Note: If you have deeply hurt or offended your mate, your apology needs to be accompanied by a "living amends"—meaning that for a period of time, before trust can be restored, you need to live like a changed person. The best place I know of to learn how to do this well, while also learning to live like a forgiven person, is in a 12-step program. (Overcomers Outreach is a 12-step program I helped to start that meets in churches all over the country. If you'd like more information, you may find a meeting place close to you at www. overcomersoutreach.org.)

A POWERFUL THREE-STEP METHOD
TO HELP YOU FORGIVE YOUR MATE

(Parts of the following method are borrowed from author Byron Katie, whose process of self-inquiry has been emotionally freeing for many. I do not believe that this method works for major offenses as well as it does for minor ones, but most of the resentment that builds up in marriages is definitely of the minor variety. It's not a perfect tool, and I don't agree with all of Byron Katie's beliefs, many of which are controversial, especially to believers. However, I owe her gratitude for the following process, which has been very helpful to many couples who are stuck in routine resentment and can't get out.)[1]

1. Write down your mate's offense. Don't hold back; write it all down. Ask yourself, *Is it true?* Then, *Can I be 100 percent sure that the thoughts I'm thinking about this person hurting me are true?*
2. Think about your grievance story. Which version of the old country song "Somebody Done Me Wrong Song" have you been playing over and over? What's the story of how your spouse hurt you that you could tell without any prompting because you have it so well memorized?
3. Ask yourself, *How would I feel about my mate if I were able to simply let go of and drop that story?* Then, here's the magic question: *Is there another way I could look at or tell that story that would be just as true, but a lot less emotionally painful?* Take your time here.

Let me give you an example to help spur your creative juices. Mandy's husband, Todd, forgot their sixth anniversary. Her grievance story went like this: "By forgetting our anniversary, Todd showed how little our love and our marriage meant to him. He didn't even have the brain space or the love for me to write the date down or remember our wedding day. I was so hurt as I waited all day, hoping and praying he'd remember. Expecting that maybe he'd surprise me. When I finally went to bed and told him what he'd done, he felt terrible, but I turned my back and cried myself to sleep. I don't know how I can let go of the pain of that day."

Mandy's therapist asked her, "Mandy, how do you feel when you tell this story?"

"Angry, furious, hurt. Unloved. Not valued. Like a knot as tight as can be is in my stomach."

The therapist nodded. "Is there another story you could tell about this incident? One that is perhaps just as true but a little more understanding and kind toward Todd? Would you try a different version and let's see how it feels?"

So Mandy sighed and then thought a bit and said, "I was so excited about our anniversary, but rather than remind Todd that it was coming up, I just thought I'd test him to see if he would remember it on his own. He rarely remembers dates of special occasions. So in a way, I guess I set him up for failure. I could have reminded him earlier in the week or that morning, and if I did, he would have planned something special, complete with a sweet card. He proves he loves me every day by word and deed. He felt terrible for forgetting and worse for hurting me. Instead of offering him the grace that God gives me daily, I punished him. It hurt both of us. I could offer him a do-over date, wipe the slate clean, and celebrate our anniversary next week."

"Now," said the therapist, "how do you feel when you share this version of the story?"

"Relaxed, loving, and better about myself and Todd. I feel free."

"Is there any good reason you can think of not to exchange story number two for story number one, since they are both just as true? Any reason to hold on to a story that makes you feel terrible and hateful rather than one that makes you feel loving and merciful?"

Mandy shook her head and smiled.

Be kind and compassionate to one another, forgiving each other,
just as in Christ God forgave you. (Eph. 4:32 NIV)

Granted, not all spousal offenses are as easy to forgive as a good husband's accidentally forgetting an anniversary. Some stories—like forgiving a spouse's adultery—involve such pain and betrayal that you'll need some professional guidance to wade through that devastating storm. And the offending mate will need to show remorse and live a long season of changed behavior for the marriage to mend.

However, in most marriages, it isn't the big things that kill it. It is the little resentments, one on top of another that pile up and suck the life out of your love. Thankfully, many marriages can be revived by many little acts of kindness, patience, and forgiveness piled one on top of the other.

Why Forgiveness Is Good for Your Brain

Lack of forgiveness can hurt your brain and body in more ways than you may realize. Though forgiveness feels like you are setting someone else free—it is also about setting yourself and your emotional health free.

Here are ten ugly things that happen to your body when you hang on to a grudge:

1. Physically, the body is in a state of stress.
2. Muscles tighten, causing imbalances or pain in the neck, back, and limbs.
3. Blood flow to the joints is restricted, making it more difficult for the blood to remove wastes from the tissues and reducing the supply of oxygen and nutrients to the cells.
4. Normal processes of repair and recovery from injury or arthritis are impaired.
5. Clenching of the jaws contributes to problems with teeth and jaw joints.
6. Headaches can become a problem. Chronic pain may get worse.
7. Blood flow to the heart is constricted.

8. Digestion is impaired.
9. Breathing may become more difficult.
10. Anger can seriously impair the immune system, increasing the risk of infections and illness.

Additionally, Dr. Fred Luskin, who started the Forgiveness Project at Stanford University and is the author of *Forgive for Good*, found that when the body releases certain enzymes during anger and stress, cholesterol and blood pressure levels go up—not a good long-term position to put the body in. On the other hand, forgiveness has been shown to lower blood pressure naturally. The bottom line is that simmering resentments may be undoing many of the positive things you are doing to improve your brain and body.

In one study, people who focused on a personal grudge had elevated blood pressure and heart rates, as well as increased muscle tension and feelings of being less in control. When asked to imagine forgiving the person who had hurt them, the participants said they felt more positive and relaxed and thus, the changes dissipated. Other studies have shown that forgiveness has positive effects on psychological health too.[2]

HONESTY

What do you think of when you think of a person of integrity? I used to think it was someone who was holy or near-perfect.

Forget that definition. *Integrity* comes from the root word *congruent* and it means, in a nutshell, to be the same inside as you are outside. There's no duplicity of character where you say one thing, but really think another. Or where you are telling your mate one thing while living a secret life on the inside or simply on the sidelines.

A truly integrated person is someone who, like Popeye, "ams what I ams." There's a sticky side to honesty, and that is that it needs to be wrapped up in kindness and timed with patience, especially in marriage. So don't hear me saying that every thought that flies through your head must be expressed. But it does mean that your mate can trust you to tell the truth and live the truth . . . in love.

When you or your mate is hiding your truest self from each other, how can there be real authentic intimacy? If you are afraid to talk honestly about problems or issues, your marriage may be experiencing "off-the-table-itis"— where one spouse has basically told the other, "I don't want to discuss this matter any further," leaving the partner feeling unheard and emotionally abandoned. The result is that one feels forced into masking his or her true self in order to keep the peace.

> *Integrity is telling myself the truth.*
> *And honesty is telling the truth to other people.*
> —Spencer Johnson

Dan says that he felt this way in his first marriage, and the frustration sent him into a ten-year chronic depression. "My wife let it be known, clearly and in no uncertain terms, that sex for us would happen once a week, on Friday night, and not to bother her any other time. Needless to say, this scheduled appointment felt more clinical than passionate to me, but by Friday, I was too desperate for relief to be picky about passion. Not the best situation for a young husband to learn and practice how to be a world-class lover.

"For me to even hint of desire on a Wednesday or, God forbid, a Tuesday, would be to have broken her rules. When I told her that my sexual rhythm was more like two to three times a week, I got the answer, 'Come on, Dan! Most husbands are lucky to get it once a week. You can wait.'

"I never felt so stuck. To please my wife I had to pretend I didn't want sex unless it was on Friday night *only*. However, my hormones, as a young, virile husband, were screaming something else. I literally felt a split within my soul. A despair that I could not name at that time began to simmer within. Depression—what I learned later was 'anger turned inward'—set in, as I knew I could not bring up the topic of wanting and needing sex more often without being reminded that the rules had been stated and set in stone. There would be no further discussion on the topic.

"Eventually I began acting out in unhealthy ways that were against my truest character. Between her withholding and my inability to 'practice regular celibacy' in a marriage relationship, our marriage ended a few years after the kids left home.

"Five years later I remarried. And in this marriage, I feel incredible free-dom. No hiding! Just happiness. I can breathe and exhale—and be real. We both talk about our sexual needs and desires with each other, and our love wants nothing more than to please and satisfy the other. And it's not just about sex; we both feel we can talk about any subject and be deeply heard and respected. A compromise or agreement is not hard to find when two people encourage honest communication in an atmosphere of love."[3]

Indeed, marriages that foster and nurture the expression of real, authen-tic, and honest feelings are some of the most blessed on the planet.

WAYS TO FOSTER HONESTY IN MARRIAGE

1. Have periodic check-ins (no mind reading required).

Periodically take turns taking the temperature of your marriage. "Honey, is there anything I can do to improve as your wife?" or "Baby, is every-thing okay? You seem a little quiet, and I'm just wondering if there's anything on your mind."

The partner then needs to respond in truth. No game playing, no mind reading, and no "you should know how I feel" responses. The only way you and your mate can grow and learn and get a PhD in each other is to talk honestly, share openly, and do it like grown-ups, not kids.

2. Combine honesty with kindness.

There is no trophy for being unkind and honest. Sorry. Honest communi-cation, especially about wanting some changes in your mate or your marriage, need to be totally cocooned in love. Good timing is also essential. Wait to dis-cuss sticky subjects until your mate is well rested, fed, alert, and in a mood for sharing deeply. (This is where patience comes in.) Some couples make a once-a-month date to discuss the "state of their union"—so both come prepared to share and receive kind suggestions of ways to improve their relationship.

3. Be humble.

My friend and cowriter, Becky, says, "Whenever I come to my husband and explain that he's hurt my feelings, as long as I don't question his motives, he always says, 'Darling, I am so sorry. I would never intentionally hurt you. I may make other mistakes, but I will try not to make this one again.' He really is the most humble and secure man I know. The way he reacts when I am honest gives me such a feeling of safety. I once asked him how he can be so gracious when I'm honest about something that has hurt me, and he answered, 'Why wouldn't I want to become a better man? And how could I do that if you never told me where I could improve?' His response is so rare, but I can tell husbands out there that his ability to be humble when I am being honest has yielded an amazing marriage, a happy wife, and a wonderful life. I respect him so much and want to be more like him in this area when I am critiqued and tempted to react defensively, instead of maturely absorbing how I can improve. I've realized it takes an awfully secure person to do this. I'm learning, but I have a ways to grow!"

4. Be responsive.

When your mate is honest about his or her needs, desires, or wants, as much as it is within your power (and as long as it doesn't clash with your values), do your best to change, help, or improve. I don't mean that you have to become a different person. In fact, if your mate is using "honesty" as a hoop for you to constantly have to jump through to get his approval, he is abusing the concept.

But if your spouse asks you to help with the kids, and it is within your power to lighten her load, ask her exactly how you can most be of help (in a kind tone). Get specific. If she says that she'd love some help getting them to bed at night, then talk about exactly what part you can play, and offer a few suggestions. "Would you like me to get them bathed and in their jammies? Read them a book?" Then, here's the hard part. Follow up and just *do it*. When you are consistent in following up on promises, you are showing her what a man of integrity she has married. And if you can't keep your promises, then go back to the table and talk about adjusting expectations in a kind and loving way.

5. Be a spouse of grace.

If you want your kids to be honest with you, then you've got to make it easy for them to tell the truth, right? The same is true in a marriage. Your mate needs to know that when he gets up the courage to tell you he just ran into the mailbox, forgot to mail the electric bill, or spilled grape juice on the white carpet in the dining room, you aren't going to freak out, yell, or lecture. That you'll take a deep breath and say something like, "Well, it was just a mistake, and I make them too. Let's see what we can do together to fix the problem. I'm on your team." Give grace to your mate when he confesses a mistake, and you'll usually get a more honest spouse.

Psychologist Carl Rogers emphasized creating an environment of "positive regard" in helping his clients to be genuine with themselves and with him. In fact, he said that any person who helps another to be more integrated (that is, the same on the inside as the outside) is acting as a therapist. Have you ever been with someone who was so accepting of you in an environment of kindness that you emotionally put your feet up and completely relaxed, were able to be as real as can be, with no worries about sharing your true thoughts? Wasn't it wonderful?

Wouldn't you love to give this gift to your mate? Wouldn't you love to receive it from your spouse? Love not only "tells the truth" but it also creates the conditions of nonjudgment and love where the truth can be easily told.

Word of warning: There are some men and women who have a duplicitous personality no matter how much you employ the techniques above. There are some men or women who lie and deceive almost as sport to see what they can get away with. If you suspect you are married to a compulsive liar, get some professional counseling right away. Because, Houston, you've got a real problem on your hands, and you'll need some help. It is also advisable to tell your therapist that your mate is really, really good at creating an impression of honesty, but that you've got proof about his or her trail of lies.

Why Being Honest Is Good for Your Brain

When people begin to be dishonest about themselves or lie to cover up mistakes or failures to their mate, something painful occurs deep inside the brain. Lies and masking literally change the brain over time. It feels like an inner dissonance, where you feel you are becoming two personalities—the one inside and the one you present to your spouse—almost, if you will, a sort of schizophrenia of the soul.

Lying or feeling compelled to mask your true feelings in a close relationship causes stress like you wouldn't believe. If you have a healthy prefrontal cortex and a working conscience, then pretending to be someone you are not causes internal stress (stress that can be picked up on a lie detector) that will eventually manifest itself in aches and pains—headaches, stomachaches, backaches, and worse. Depression and anxiety can go through the roof when one mate is hiding his or her true self or a big mistake from the other. The cleansing act of confessing our "sins" to each other in a place of grace is one of the healthiest balms to the human soul. (*Sin* literally means "like an arrow missing the mark," which I think is a great description. It means we've missed or strayed from God's best for us in a situation.)

As a therapist, I often feel more like a priest in a confessional. Sometimes all a client really needs to begin to get well is to tell one understanding, non-judging human soul the truth about his or her life and to know I won't (can't!) tell anyone else . . . and that I won't respond with shock or judgment. If Christians could do this for each other more often, I might be out of business (which would be fine by me).

> *Speaking the truth in love, we will in all things grow up . . .*
> (Eph. 4:15 NIV)

Warning: If you have been unfaithful in the past and long to clear your conscience by telling your spouse your offenses, I urge you not to do this without first finding and talking to a Christian therapist you trust. You'll need help on how to share this with your mate, to discuss the motives for your sharing, and if you decide to tell the truth, your mate will need the support of a therapist as well.

THE PERFECT MARRIAGE

From the perspective of my own marriage and from hundreds of couples whom I've counseled over the past thirty-plus years, here are the qualities that I find in the happiest marriages, the top 10 percent, the blessed few.

1. Both partners are proactive about their passion.

One partner can hold up the marriage for a period of time while the other one gets to be a little crazy-busy or is going through a bad spell.

But not for years on end.

It takes *two* trying their best to *be* their best, to be the blessed few. Do not coast on your partner's efforts or you will, eventually, be coasting alone.

2. Their sexuality and spirituality are robust.

The happiest couples make love regularly and enthusiastically, realizing it is one of God's gifts to ease some of the challenges of a marriage. Couples who celebrate their sexuality together tend to overlook a *lot* more little faults in each other. Most men cannot think clearly unless they make love regularly with their wives. "My husband always 'resurrects' about every third day," says one wife with a chuckle. "He gets a look in his eye that is singly focused on being naked with me! I actually see his clockworklike need for sex as God's way of making sure we get regular intimate time with each other, skin to skin, soul to soul. It's such a creative way of keeping busy humans connected." As a marriage therapist, I always breathe a happy sigh of relief and joy when couples in trouble begin connecting sexually again. It usually means more playfulness, more patience with the other, and a better ability to see their marriage from a more positive point of view. Sure makes my job easier from this point on.

3. They take responsibility for bringing their best brains to the marriage.

If a brain imbalance is creating problems in a marriage, the husbands and wives who agree to get help have a much greater chance of saving, improving, or enhancing their relationship. They are also personally much happier. I recently saw a TV show where one of the characters was a soldier returning from Iraq. He refused to get help for his post-traumatic stress until he woke up from a bad dream with his hands around the throat of the girl he loved. At that moment he realized that his mental "issues" were literally killing the person he loved. Then he got motivated to get some help for his brain issues. This is such a great metaphor for why it is important to get your brain balanced. Not only will you sleep easier and be happier, but you will stop unintentionally killing your mate by breaking his or her heart.

4. They are reeds of God's love to each other.

Nurture the spiritual arts of kindness, patience, forgiveness, and honesty (wrapped in kindness). You may want to rotate these four attributes to focus on for one week out of every month. For example, week one, you can pray for, read about, and practice random acts of kindness to your spouse. Week two, you can pray for, read about, meditate on, and practice patience and so on until these attributes literally become a part of who you are as a person and as a mate.

Now, if you both do all of the above, will you have a perfect marriage?
I wish.

I have to say that I've seen some amazing marriages in my life. But I have never seen a perfect marriage because every marriage has these two little problems: they are made up of two flawed and often selfish human beings. There's something in all of us that longs to experience love perfectly, and you know what? Someday we will. I love how Paul finishes out 1 Corinthians 13 by pointing us toward heaven where we'll experience a love so lavish that all earthly love, no matter how great, will pale in comparison.

> We don't yet see things clearly. We're squinting in a fog, peering through a mist. But it won't be long before the weather clears and the sun shines bright! We'll see it all then, see it all as clearly as God sees us, knowing him directly just as he knows us! But for right now, until that completeness, we have three things to do to lead us toward that consummation: Trust steadily in God, hope unswervingly, love extravagantly. And the best of the three is love. (vv. 12–13 MSG)

So my friends, as I close this book, my prayer for every reader is that you will be part of the blessed few who have learned the secrets of loving each other extravagantly—giving each other a little taste of heaven's love on earth.

I typically sign off all my newsletters and books with a nod to Garrison Keillor, whose characters so well describe the community in which I grew up. So this is the news from Brea, "where all the women are strong, the men are good-looking, and the kids are above average."

And where all the married couples who've read this book are having a very hard time keeping their hands off each other.

The Joy Diet

The good news is that what is good for your mood is good for your brain, good for your heart, and good for your weight!

Fat Heads

One of the surprising and perhaps most delightful bits of brand-new research is that two kinds of saturated fats—from whole milk products and butter, as well as coconut oil—do not affect your body negatively when taken in normal doses as do some of the other saturated fats (corn oil, vegetable oil, and so on). And, in fact, they add the yummy touch of comfort and taste in small portions to calm, soothe, and lubricate your brain. (See *The Mood Cure* and Nina Planck's *Real Food*—both excellent books that speak to the subject of healthy fats with news that may surprise and delight you. Another fascinating book on the physiology of eating quality food with mindful, relaxed pleasure is *The Slow-Down Diet* by Marc David.)

When our nation went fat-free for a decade (remember the T-Factor Diet fad of the '80s and '90s?), we not only got fatter but also more depressed . . . in droves. We were feeding our bodies more sugar and less healthy fat, creating one giant brain crisis. Your brain is largely made up of fat and, therefore, needs regular amounts of it in small doses to keep the membranes nourished and healthy and for you to remain calm and clear.

Farm-Raised Folks

The old-fashioned, natural way of eating—a lean protein, a glass of milk, some veggies and whole grains, and fruit as snacks and dessert—was pretty much the best diet our country ever had for nourishing the brain. Basically, anything that brings us *back to the farm*—the way a family would eat if they had to grow their own food, milk their own cows, churn their own butter, and kill their own chickens—seems to be the best diet for the brain after all.

And of course, adding in the exercise of plowing and harvesting and milking and churning to your daily routine couldn't hurt.

Looking back on my childhood, I was raised on a Minnesota Farm Diet, where we grew and ate our own veggies and always had a large freezer full of what would now be called *organic* beef. Our neighbors, who had time to go fishing in the Land of 10,000 Lakes, would bring us fresh fish. Milk came straight from the cow each day. (We did pasteurize it first.) Actually, there was very little purchased at the store.

How we can improve today on that classic diet is to emphasize even more fish than beef and get really creative with fruits and veggies until we are eating a quart of them a day. Also, by adopting the Mediterranean's heart-healthy use of olive oil in our cooking, we are protecting our brains and hearts.

For those who can tolerate milk and milk products, raise your frosty mug and enjoy that milk mustache again. In studies where people ate the same amount of calories but half the group had a good amount of dairy in their diet, the dairy eaters lost more weight and were healthier and felt more satisfied overall. If you can't tolerate milk, you can try lactose tablets or yogurt, substitute soy products, or try organic, hormone-free milk products. You may be surprised to discover that it wasn't the milk but the hormones in it that caused negative reactions.

A Word on Organic

I know it is expensive. However, the fewer toxins your body has to process, the happier your liver will be and the more vitamins you'll be getting. By shopping for what's on sale and stocking up if you can, it isn't hard these days to eat organic, at least partially organic, on a budget. Trader Joe's and Sunflower Market often offer great deals on organic produce, dairy, and meat. And most major grocery chains have jumped into the organic pond, cutting costs for all of us. It is safer to eat the nonorganic produce if it is thick skinned—such as bananas or navel oranges or pineapples. In fact, most tropical fruits are generally less exposed to toxic chemicals. So use your budget to buy organic berries, peaches, apples, and other thin-skinned produce.

Also, if you are consuming a lot of one product—for example, milk or hamburger—try to use the organic or antibiotic-free brands. Sam's Club carries milk products that are hormone free (though not organic) . . . and at a very reasonable cost.

Buy bags of frozen organic berries in bulk when they go on sale because they will last a long time and can be used to make ice cream–like frozen desserts in seconds with the addition of a little yogurt and honey in a blender. Sprinkle with toasted nuts or wheat germ and you'll never know you aren't eating Italian gelato. A high-quality blender, the best you can afford, will be an investment in your family's health too. The Vita-Mix brand is expensive; however, you can toss a whole apple or carrot in there—complete with all its fiber—and it goes down in a silky, pureed juice form, smoothly and deliciously. You can toss in a carton of cottage cheese and blend it on high until absolutely smooth, and it tastes like sour cream or cream cheese, only with so much more protein and less fat. Add a little maple syrup and vanilla, and use like whipped cream on warmed fruit (pears heated with fruit juice and cinnamon are nice); then sprinkle with granola or nuts, and you have an amazing dessert that is full of protein and fiber.

When you do decide to sweeten a sauce, smoothie, hot tea, or other recipe, try real maple syrup, honey, agave nectar (90 percent fructose but low glycemic), stevia, or a spoonful of frozen apple juice or white grape juice concentrate instead of refined white sugar or artificial sweeteners. A little goes a long way and does less harm to your blood/brain balance. The absolute worst (and commonly used) sugar you can put in your body is corn syrup—it gets to your blood even faster than table sugar. Try to avoid buying products that use this as an ingredient whenever you can.

Now to the brain food!

LEAN PROTEIN

Fish

Salmon, especially Alaskan salmon caught in the wild (the farmed variety is not as rich in omega-3 fatty acids), tuna, mackerel, and herring (which are *oilier* fishes), and all fish—mahimahi, cod, orange roughy, and tilapia—are nutritious, full of protein, and easy to digest. Once you find a few recipes you like, you'll get hooked on the way you feel after you eat fish.

Fish tacos are a great place to start if fish has never been your favorite food. Or just pat any of the spices you love along with a sprinkle of salt and pepper into fish filets and sauté on medium-high in olive oil (finish in the microwave or oven if the outside gets crispy before the insides are done). Make fish nuggets by rolling small fish chunks in a thick teriyaki sauce, and then again in nuts or sesame seeds, and bake at 350 degrees for about 15 minutes. Or roll filets in egg whites, then in seasoned bread crumbs (Japanese panko crumbs are incredibly light and crunchy), and sauté . . . delicious!

Note: To purchase the safest, most toxin- and mercury-free fish, of particular concern for pregnant and nursing women and children, you can download a handy wallet-sized safest-fish list at http://www.coopamerica.org/programs/livinggreen/safeseafood.cfm.

Poultry

Chicken and turkey, with a little skin (crisped!), is okay for you, especially if you are suffering from a low mood; it will help the uptake of nutrients that calm your brain (see *The Mood Cure* and *Real Food*). One of the worst things about no-fat and low-fat diets is that they are terrible for moods and disastrous for the brain. Every brain cell in your body needs fat to function. The best fats? Olive oil (keep it on your counter near where you cook; it is a very stable oil that doesn't go rancid easily), a little real butter now and again, and full-fat coconut milk (the fat rises to the top and is delicious to cook with). You can get cans of coconut milk in the Asian section of any grocery store. It makes an amazing addition to smoothies: mix with ice and pineapple for a healthy piña colada.

Avoid trans fat, which, thankfully, has become easier to do. With increased awareness of trans fat dangers, groceries, restaurants, and even fast-food eateries are making changes toward using healthier oils.

Alternatives

- Meat: Lean beef and pork
- Eggs: Enriched DHA eggs are best
- Tofu and soy products: Whenever possible, choose organically raised. Don't overdo soy because of how it affects hormones, but one-half cup to one cup a day is good for you.
- Dairy products: Low-fat, not no-fat, dairy, particularly when you

are trying to balance low moods. It's easier to be satisfied on a half cup of dairy with some fat in it than on one cup without any fat. If you are feeling happy, it's okay to use no-fat dairy again, as long as you are getting olive oil and fish oil in your diet.

- Beans: Especially garbanzo beans (hummus is a good way to get these) and lentils (also a good carbohydrate source)
- Nuts and seeds: Especially walnuts (also listed under fats). Toasting them just a minute or two and sprinkling with a pinch of sea salt really brings out their flavors. Great in salads.

COMPLEX CARBOHYDRATES—FRUITS, VEGGIES, AND GRAINS, OH MY!

Try getting four cups of fruits and veggies (one quart) a day, and if you manage to do that—plus get your protein, a little fat, and some grains—you can't gain weight and will probably lose weight if needed. All that fiber fills you up, and there's just not room for donuts. (If you can slowly work your way up to consuming 35 grams of fiber per day from a variety of sources, you'll not only feel great but also find it easier to lose or maintain your weight.) And soon, the desire for donuts will fade anyway. Two tricks: make a smoothie out of your fruit requirement; eat salad or veggie-based soup to help with your daily veggie consumption.

Eat from the Rainbow

Mixing colors is a good way to think about healthy fruits and vegetables. Strive to eat red things (strawberries, raspberries, cherries, red peppers, and tomatoes), yellow things (squash, yellow peppers, small portions of bananas, and peaches), blue things (blueberries), purple things (plums), orange things (oranges, tangerines, and yams), green things (peas, spinach, and broccoli), and so on.

Here are some of the best brain-healthy fruits and veggies and whole grains:

- Berries. Especially blueberries (Dr. Amen calls them *brain berries*), raspberries, strawberries, blackberries. Use one cup of frozen mixed berries in a smoothie as a base for a fabulous-tasting, nutrition-dense shake. Use one to three tablespoons of protein powder—nonflavored whey is great; you can't taste it—and you've got breakfast or lunch in a cup. Or just leave berries whole and defrost just slightly, add a little drizzle of pure maple syrup and a tablespoon of half-and-half. Delicious.

- Oranges, lemons, limes, grapefruit. Get an orange juicer—a cheap plastic hand juicer will do—and squeeze your fresh juice in the morning. You'll get hooked. Citrus peel is loaded with antioxidants, so investing in a good citrus zester will not only add punch to your cooking but nutrition to your meals.

- Cherries. Good for arthritis too—100 percent cherry juice is a common aid to those who suffer with joint pain.

- Peaches, plums.

- Broccoli, cauliflower, brussels sprouts, cabbage.

- Oats, whole wheat, wheat germ. Oatmeal needs to be the slower-cooking kind because instant has a higher glycemic index since the manufacturer has broken down the fiber to speed cooking time and basically made it a refined carbohydrate. I don't leave the long-cooking oatmeal on for very long because I like it less mushy. Same goes for bread. Look for at least three grams of fiber. Try the new double-fiber breads!

- Red or yellow peppers. Much higher in vitamin C than green peppers—green peppers are simply unripe red peppers. Try roasting red peppers yourself; just put them over the open flame of your gas burner until they are black all over. Put in a plastic baggie to let the skin loosen in the steam. Then rub off the skin and there you go—roasted red peppers ready to add flavor to any meal or soup.

- Pumpkin, squash, carrots.

- Spinach. Works wonderfully as a salad or a cooked vegetable and adds fiber and nutrients.

- Tomatoes. Both fresh and canned are great. Actually, tomato paste and sauce are richer in some cancer-fighting nutrients than fresh tomatoes.

- Yams/sweet potatoes.

- Kale or any deep-green leafy veggie. Kale is one of the most nutrient-dense veggies in the produce section, but how many of us have even tried it? (Hint: try removing the stems first.) If you cook kale in water, toss out the water, and you'll eliminate any bitterness. But it is delicious sautéed, without the stems, in a little olive oil with mushrooms, salt and pepper, and a dash of nutmeg. Deglaze the pan when it's done with a little dash of wine, cook a few more minutes, and serve.
- Brown rice and other whole grains. Leftover brown rice with dried fruit, nuts, and a little cinnamon or honey and a little milk makes a tasty hot cereal. Bulgur or brown rice can make a wonderful pilaf—toss in toasted nuts, some dried cranberries, and any herbs you like, and you've got a tasty, nutritious side dish. Don't forget to use grains in cold, summer salads. Tabouli (bulgur with cucumbers, parsley, tomatoes, garlic, lemon juice, and olive oil) is always refreshing, but you can create any number of grain-based salads by mixing equal parts grain and chopped fresh veggies or beans, a handful of herbs, and your favorite olive oil–based salad dressing.

Note: Almost any veggie tastes amazing steamed and then tossed with a little bit of butter, a squeeze of fresh citrus (orange, lemon, or lime), and a dash of salt and pepper. Also, try tossing a bowl of cut-up veggies in Italian dressing and olive oil; then spread on a cookie sheet and slow-roast for 30 minutes at 300 to 350 degrees or until tender and almost caramelized. Try roasting sweet potato wedges or rounds like this. Yummm!

FATS

- Avocados (guacamole!)
- Extra-virgin cold-pressed olive oil
- Olives
- Salmon (also listed under protein)
- Nuts and nut butter: especially walnuts, macadamia nuts, Brazil nuts, pecans, and almonds (also listed under protein)
- Real butter in reasonable amounts: Just a tad will go a long way to

make food taste better. Clarifed butter or ghee can also be used in cooking and won't burn easily.

LIQUIDS

- Water
- Green or black tea
- Milk: Calcium is good for your bones, and studies show that dairy is also an aid in weight loss. The no- or low-fat versions will help keep calories down, but you need to make sure you are getting enough fat in your system through olive oil and nuts and other good sources to optimize mood and brain function. If not, go ahead and enjoy the full-fat versions of milk products. And if you need to gain a little weight, by all means enjoy whole milk products, especially if you don't have any dairy allergies.
- Juices: Used in small amounts, unsweetened fruit juice can make a good base for smoothies. But there's so much sugar in most juices that I would not recommend them without the fiber included to slow down the absorption of sugar. So go ahead and squeeze juice from an orange, but scrape in the pulp as well. Or enjoy whole fruit smoothies instead.

PROBIOTICS = HEALTHIER GUT, HEALTHIER BRAIN

In his book *The Brain Diet,* author Alan C. Logan advocates using probiotics to help keep the gut healthy, improve immunity, and ultimately boost brain health. There are many good products to help "reseed" the gut with friendly bacteria, but one of the best researched and most easily accessible is the DanActive yogurt drinks. They are small, tasty, and may help keep inflammation in your body down, resulting in fewer illnesses, fewer digestive problems, and yes, ultimately even a healthier brain.[1] (For the peer-reviewed research on this helpful new product, see www.dan-active.com/danactive_scientific.html.)

Common Questions About
SPECT Scans

1. Does everyone need a scan? No. Often the Amen Brain System Checklist included in this book can help guide us to the right medications or supplements to try, if needed. We look at the degree of angst and pain that a person is in, the history of what he has tried before, and several other factors. Often we can be of help by using therapy or coaching techniques and suggesting supplements or medications that his healthcare professional may want to consider.

I am not a medical doctor; I am just a trained therapist who has deeply studied the area of brain imaging and picked up all I could possibly learn from Dr. Amen, the pioneer of this research. So I am only one piece of the total health puzzle. The book *The Tipping Point* talks about a personality called The Connector, and that really fits my personality. I may be able to help you, but if I cannot, I know a good list of healthcare professionals who probably can.

2. When does a person need a SPECT scan? When your situation is complicated and you are not seeing improvement or when there's a suspicion of past brain injury or trauma that could be affecting behavior, a scan would be beneficial. When we suspect the temporal lobes may be a problem, using a SPECT scan really helps us diagnose exactly what's happening and determines the order in which we will treat brain issues. Also, in cases of complicated ADD, we use it where the normal stimulant protocol isn't working or is making things worse. A scan can help us with much better accuracy to help you help yourself.

3. Aren't SPECT scans expensive? In a word, yes, they can be. (At this writing, anywhere from $1,500 to $5,000, depending on how many scans are taken and the protocol needed.) Insurance may cover some of the costs; however, most scanning centers—including the Amen Clinics—require you to pay first and let the insurance company reimburse you. But if you (or your therapist or doctor) suspects you really need a brain scan, there may be ways to help reduce costs or divide payments with a payment plan. Sometimes it does help to ask yourself, *What is it worth for me to know exactly where my brain may be misfiring and exactly how to help it?*

The easiest way to see if our office can help you is to contact us at www .henslinandassoc.com or 1-714-256-HOPE, where we can assess your individual needs and situation and let you know how we can best help within your circumstances.

4. Where can I find a healthcare provider in my area who is familiar with SPECT scans and understands the benefit of Dr. Amen's work? Go to www.amenclinics.com/ac/referrals. You can enter in your location, and a number of healthcare professionals who are familiar with Dr. Amen's approach will pop up.

Here are some more common Q & A's from Dr. Amen's Web site:

1. What is SPECT imaging? Single Photon Emission Computed Tomography imaging, also called brain SPECT imaging, is a nuclear medicine procedure that evaluates cerebral blood flow. SPECT is easy to understand. It evaluates areas of the brain that work well, areas of the brain that work too hard, and areas of the brain that do not work hard enough. The information from the scans, along with a detailed clinical history, helps us understand the underlying brain patterns associated with our patients' problems and helps to pinpoint the right treatment to balance brain function.

2. What is the procedure? You will be placed in a quiet room, and a small IV line will be inserted into your arm. For the concentration study, you will take a fifteen-minute computerized test of attention and focus. Three or four minutes into performing the test, the imaging solution will be injected through the IV, and then you will complete the test. For the baseline study, you will be instructed to sit quietly. Several minutes later, the imaging solution will be injected through the IV. After the injection, you will lie on the imaging table, and the SPECT camera will slowly rotate around your head, taking images of brain blood flow. (You are not placed inside a tube.) The time on the table is approximately eighteen minutes.

3. What is the injection, and are there side effects? Since a SPECT scan is a nuclear medicine procedure, it requires the injection of a very small amount of a radioisotope through a small needle inserted into a vein in the arm. The medicine we inject is not a dye; therefore, people typically do not have allergic responses to it.

4. Does the injected substance you use contain iodine? No, it does not. It is not a dye or a contrast agent, such as those used in CTs or MRIs. It is a radioactive tracer ("radiotracer" or "tracer"). This is a very important distinction: in CT, the term *dye* or *contrast agent* refers to an injected compound that typically contains iodine and is used to enhance an X-ray or CT image. Severe reactions can occur in some patients who receive these iodine-containing substances. A history of bad reactions to CT dyes, however, does not mean that a patient will have a bad reaction to the tracers we use. Adverse reactions to the radiotracers used at the Amen Clinics are so rare that hospital nuclear medicine departments typically do not stock the drugs given to patients with a history of reactions to iodine-based contrast agents.

The radiotracers injected at the Amen Clinics do contain a substance called *methylene blue*. This substance is a dye but is not the same kind of dye as the iodine-containing X-ray and CT contrast agents. It functions as a preservative and helps the radiotracer stay in its compounded form. There are no serious allergic or adverse effects that we know of associated with the administration of methylene blue.

5. Is there radiation involved, and how safe is it? How safe is it for children? The amount of radiation exposure from one brain SPECT scan is comparable to one-half to two-thirds of a brain CAT (CT) scan (about 0.7 to 1.0 rem). According to the Health Physics Society, the radiation dose of two SPECT scans is well below the cut-off level (10 rem) for any potential or observable health risks. Furthermore, according to the National Institutes of Health, research data does not show children to have any increased cancer risks from low-level radiation.

6. Are there any risks from the radiation you get from a SPECT scan? Minimal risks, if any, may exist. The radiation from a SPECT scan is considered a standard medical procedure. Last year in the United States, there were nearly twenty million nuclear medicine procedures done on children and adults. Please see http://interactive.snm.org/index.cfm?PageID=5574&RPID= 10 for a thorough discussion.

7. Do I have to be off medication, and for how long? We prefer to scan patients on as little medication as possible, if not off it completely. We realize this is not always practical depending on your circumstances. Stimulant medications need to be stopped four days prior to the first scan. Any other decrease or removal of medications needs to be done in consultation with your treating physician.

For more information about SPECT and Amen Clinics,
go to www.amenclinic.com.

New Hope: Men and Sexual Addiction

1. How many men do you suppose have some kind of problem with Internet porn or other sexual addiction? How widespread is the problem?

Dr. Patrick Carnes, the nation's most respected researcher in this area, estimates that twelve million men in the United States are sexual addicts. Some authors will uniformly say that anywhere from 40 to 60 percent of men are addicted to pornography, and that seems accurate to me. There's a wide perception that only men have sexual addictions, but women have them as well; however, women often express their lust for male attention by dressing in provocative ways or flirting dangerously. Where men tend to head to visual images, women tend to get addicted to chat rooms and Internet flirtations. It is assumed that it is just men who struggle with masturbation in marriage, but many wives prefer masturbation or vibrators to sexual intimacy with their husbands as well.

I have been working with sexual addiction with both men and women since the mid-1970s, and I can assure you that lust is not just a "guy problem." We are also having an increasing number of calls in the last five years about teens who are sexually addicted.

2. How do sexual images affect the brain and cause it to become addicted?

Emotionally arousing images imprint and alter the brain and trigger an instant involuntary but lasting biochemical memory trail. It takes just a fraction of a second for the image to pass from the eyes to the brain. This trail of multisensory images also leaves a neurochemical and hormonal imprint—experienced as lust—that gives a high or rush not unlike any stimulating drug.

Once the images are "on file" in the brain, the slightest visual trigger or internal thought can set off an obsession with that internal image. I've seen men create arguments or conflicts with their spouse so they can create a "reason" to act out their sexual addiction. ("My wife got mad at me, so what could I do?")

Sadly, because of the Internet, children ages ten and above are the fastest-growing population of new sexual addicts. Children left alone to journey the Internet superhighway do not have the judgment or impulse control to say no to viewing vivid and explicit images and, sadly, they can get hooked very quickly. Guard your kids!

3. From what I've heard, getting truly free of a sexual addiction has proven to be one of the most challenging problems for men, and for the therapists and pastors trying to help them out of the trap.

Lust is difficult to overcome for a number of reasons. In the SPECT Brain Imaging Scans that we have done for more than ten years now, we have found that in every single case of sexual addiction (male or female) there was an injury in the prefrontal cortex. As you may remember from the chapter on the Scattered Lover, the prefrontal cortex, the presidential control center of the brain, plays a significant role in judgment, impulse control, fore-thought, planning, and conscience.

When we help optimize brain function, there is more access to impulse control, allowing for that all-important split-second pause between stimulus and response. So the relapse rate is significantly decreased. Many men and women are just one medication or supplement away from having better self-control.

There are many wonderful Christian ministries and support groups, such as Celebrate Recovery, that help the sexual addict today. If a man or woman continues to relapse into acting out sexual lust in unhealthy ways, we encourage that person to attend Sexaholics Anonymous (www.sa.org) in addition to whatever program he or she is involved in. The SA groups in Southern California are 80 to 90 percent Christian men. The program tools of sponsorship, working through the 12-steps, doing service, and attending meetings are very strong and helpful. Sexaholics Anonymous has also been conducting and developing its program since the midseventies, so they have a longer history of success. We have seen many successful stories of lives and marriages freed from this addiction through this program.

As is the case of all addictions, your best chance of success is to work on healing from several approaches: (1) the biochemical/brain health, (2) a strong support group, and (3) the support of a therapist to help you look at your history and work through personal issues that may have led to your vulnerability to sexual addiction.

4. I've heard it often takes up to three years of intense help, and even then, the changes are often not lasting. "Every man's battle" sounds like it has turned into a war like the one in Iraq—longer, harder, and trickier than we ever realized the problem would be.

As much as I'd like to declare that a man will be totally free of or delivered from lust if he gets his brain balanced and joins a good support group, I could never promise this as a realistic outcome. Are any of us ever totally free from our sin nature? In some ways we are all lust addicts—though the object of our lust might not be sex. For some, it is food, work, alcohol, or shopping.

What I can say is that Christ promises to be with us in the second-by-second battle of lust. I can promise there will be more successes than failures for those who seek help and get it!

Lust will not be eradicated in a three-to-four day seminar or a weekend retreat. However, these are often good starting points for the journey toward freedom.

5. How can a brain scan and balancing a brain help? Does it speed up the time for getting "cured"? Does it help the "cure" to stick and last?

Again, I could not honestly participate in saying a person is "cured" of sexual addiction. Research on alcoholism years ago said that about 5 percent of all alcoholics had a dramatic spiritual experience where they never craved to drink again. Wonderful for them! However, that leaves us with the 95 percent of men and women who had to learn to stay sober one day, one minute, one second at a time, with God and the fellowship of others who struggle.

That said, balancing brain chemistry certainly does help give a person that extra split second where he can more freely choose an alternative to acting out what has now become a habitual response to lust. With the support group in place, individuals with a normally functioning prefrontal cortex can now evoke their free will and make the step to pray or walk away, or call a sponsor for emotional support.

For more than a decade we have witnessed one person after another have much more success in recovery from sexual addiction after we've helped balance their brain.

6. Which areas of the brain are usually the culprits in hard-core sexual addiction? What supplements or medications help?

Though I could not say there is just one system in the brain that plays a role in hard-core addiction, here is the pattern we see most often in SPECT scans of those who struggle with lust.

A. We almost always see a drop in perfusion (blood flow) in the prefrontal cortex, typical of ADD. When life feels too routine or boring, this type of personality will start to feel depressed or lethargic. So they will often seek experiences that elevate dopamine, which plays a role in the experience of pleasure.

Sexual addiction is just one dopamine-producing high. Gambling, playing the stock market, taking risks in business, or a high interest in extreme sports also offers a temporary rush that tickles the PFC. Once experienced, many people live for the high stimulation or adrenaline rush. And sadly, it takes more and more extreme "risking" for many people to experience the same rush. Even more sadly, addiction to artificial or extreme highs over a long period of time dampens a person's ability to feel joy over the "simple pleasures" of life.

B. Injury or lack of blood flow in the prefrontal cortex plays a part in the lack of impulse control. The person is not able to think through the consequences of his or her actions as well as someone who has a healthy PFC.

C. We often see the cingulate showing overactivity—becoming fixated or obsessed on an object or image.

D. Instability or injury in the temporal lobes may also play a role in overactive fantasizing.

There are many medications and supplements that help.

We examine and correct brain imbalances in a specific order, always beginning with the temporal lobes. (If you try to correct out of order and there is a temporal lobe injury, you can do more harm than good with medication.)

First we want to stabilize any temporal lobe imbalance with specialized medications such as Neurontin or Lamictal, depending on the presence or absence of mood swings. Supplements such as high-quality omega-3 fish oil, GABA, 5-HTP, or SAM-e can help as well, depending on the presenting issues. (With both medication and supplements, you will want to have a recommendation from a qualified physician who is familiar with SPECT imaging.)

Second, we look at the limbic and cingulate areas and balance them with antidepressant medication, if needed, or supplementation and lifestyle changes that help depression.

Finally, if we see that blood flow is low to the prefrontal cortex, we will recommend a stimulant such as Adderall, Vyvanse, Focalin, Ritalin, or Concerta. Dr. Amen has supplements that help with this area, such as Brain Vitale and NeuroStim. The amino acid tyrosine is often very helpful in milder focus problems.

7. Along with brain balancing, what else have you found works best to help men escape the sexual addiction trap? In other words, what are the best supportive helps or interventions?

- Sexaholics Anonymous for the reasons mentioned above
- Celebrate Recovery
- Jayson Graves, MFT, (blazingGrace.org) and Mark Laaser, PhD, (faithfulandtrueministries.com) are two men I admire who both are doing great work in this area.

I personally believe the best chance of finding freedom is a combination of getting to a therapist who is knowledgeable about brain chemistry and sexual addiction, who will also plug clients into the best support groups in their area.

Though some therapists suggest accountability programs to put on the computer that will send a list of "viewed sites" to a designated monitor (usually a wife or friend), I see limits to this working well long-term. First, you have to assume that the addict is only going to use a laptop or home computer. People today have access to the Internet via their cell phones and Internet cafés, and most teens are computer savvy enough to bypass most software programs. (That said, I do think that filters on computers for children work beautifully.)

Rather than spend a lot of time and effort to "avoid" thinking about the pink elephant (porn sites), I've found it more effective to help my clients get re-involved in positive pursuits. I suggest that my clients begin spending more quality time with their wives and families. Go to bed the same time as their spouses do, even if one isn't sleepy. (A small book light can let one partner read while the other dozes off.) Develop a good exercise and nutritional program to manage stress, and improve heart and brain health. Get engaged in a new, healthy, meaningful activity. I could go on, but that would be another book.

8. Would you say something to the wives of men who are addicted to porn or have visited massage parlors or prostitutes? Their self-esteem is wiped out, and many cannot imagine feeling loved or desired enough to want to make love with their husbands again. If a woman just stumbled into your office after she either caught her husband or he confessed to a sexual addiction, what would you say?

I have a list of women who have "been there" and have given me permission to hand their phone numbers out to wives who've just discovered their husbands are addicted to pornography or worse. I also encourage these wives to attend S-Anon, which is a 12-step support group for the spouses and family members of the sexual addict.

The couples who are the most successful in the recovery and restoration of their marriages are the ones where the sexual addict is attending SA, and the spouse is attending S-Anon (or similar program, such as Celebrate Recovery or Overcomers Outreach).

I find that there are several stages for the woman who just found out her husband is struggling with sexual addiction:

- Grief. Finding out her spouse is a sexual addict is like taking the heart and soul of a woman and ripping it right down the middle. It is literally a feeling of being torn apart. There needs to be time to grieve. In addition, sometimes women feel they were not enough

woman or could never meet up to the images on their husbands'
laptops. These are heart-wrenching emotions and questions that
need answers. Other women who've been there—and I, as a
therapist—can offer a great deal of support and soothing responses.

- Anger is an important stage of grief, but if inflamed and held too
  closely for too long, it can turn into a delicious feeling that does
  more harm than good. It is stimulating and empowering and gives
  such a sense of righteousness. I am not minimizing the hurt that the
  wounded spouse feels; however, anger beyond what is normal and
  necessary is no longer a healing emotion. I will work with the wives
  to help them move past destructive anger to positive solutions.

- We have found through the years that many times the spouse of a
  sexually addicted partner will have an overactive basal ganglia or
  cingulate that makes it difficult for her to let go and move on.
  So a part of helping the wife to move into forgiveness may also
  be helping to balance and calm her brain as well.

- A note for the wife: She needs to know that only her husband
  can make the choice and do the work to heal himself. She can
  be supportive and can work on her own issues, but ultimately
  her husband must take 100 percent responsibility to become a
  man of greater integrity and gather all the support he can to
  make that happen.

New Hope: Women and Hormones

Since hormones create the neurotransmitters that ultimately affect our moods, and since there is a new flux of research and interest in bio-identical hormones, I want to address some of the more common questions I am asked in this area. Hormone adjustment, for both men and women, can sometimes make a huge difference in the happiness, sex life, and emotional connection in marriage.

1. How do hormones affect brain function, and ultimately mood? Can you see hormone imbalance on a SPECT scan?

Yes and no.

Yes, you can see how hormones impact the brain on SPECT scans. One of the more fascinating scans is of a woman's brain before PMS and during PMS, usually showing an inflamed cingulate or limbic system. So in this way, yes, you can "see" how hormone fluctuations can affect brain patterns. SPECT Brain Imaging is a metabolic study, so it shows the influence of everything we eat, drink, and also how genetics influence brain function.

However, can you tell from a SPECT scan that there is a hormone imbalance and how to correct it? No, that is done through hormone or endocrine panels that you can have ordered by your physician, nurse practitioner, or physician assistant. The scan, however, may give us clues as to which hormone panels are needed.

2. When do you suspect that a woman may need to be tested for hormonal imbalance?

When I have tried therapy and ordered a SPECT scan, treating brain imbalances with medication or supplements, and there seems to be a lingering level of anxiety, depression, memory problems, or irritability, I will usually send a note to her MD requesting that a hormone panel be done. What are the red flags or clues? If a woman has polycystic ovarian disease, difficult and heavy periods, is premenopausal, in the midst of menopause, or postmenopausal, my antennae go up. One hormone that routinely gets missed by both men and women is the hormone insulin. If the man or woman is a compulsive overeater who has gained and lost the same weight over and over, usually that person is having problems with glycemic control and will need to develop a food plan that is a little higher on proteins than carbs.

Increasingly with men I am routinely requesting that they get a testosterone level done, particularly if they are over the age of fifty and are struggling with fatigue, depression, or anxiety.

3. I hear a lot about bioidentical hormone replacement. What is your opinion about this route, rather than synthetic hormone treatments?

The doctors that I refer my clients to for hormonal imbalances are specialists in their field who rely heavily on bioidenticals. The research that caused the hormone–cancer connection scare that resulted in many MDs dropping hormone replacement strategies was based on studies using synthetic hormone replacement.

Bioidentical hormones offer fresh hope for the "hormone impaired," and both Dr. Amen and I are excited about the research and the results in this area.

4. I have terrible migraines that occur around ovulation and my period. Could a bioidentical hormone cream, such as progesterone cream, help?

Yes, quite possibly a progesterone cream might be helpful. I would suggest getting your hormones tested for this and see what your levels were throughout your cycle. If progesterone doesn't help, I have found that Neurontin can be very helpful with headaches caused from either basal ganglia or temporal lobe overactivity.

Dr. Steven Hotze, the author of *Hormones, Health, and Happiness*, says, "Estrogen dominance is also a culprit in PMS headaches and migraines. One reason for this is that estrogen promotes water retention. Because the brain is confined to the fixed space of the skull, when it swells, the pressure that develops causes a headache. Estrogen also causes dilation of the blood vessels. The constriction of the blood vessels followed by rebound dilation is a key factor in migraines. Finally, estrogen dominance leads to the depletion of the mineral magnesium, which is crucial to normal blood vessel tone. Magnesium deficiency can cause a spasm of arteries in the brain. So taking 300 to 400 mg of magnesium, preferably in the evening for its calming effects, may help, along with hormonal balancing."[1]

5. Can you talk about thyroid, insulin imbalance, and adrenal/cortisol impairment?

When do you suggest a client have these checked? Are there red flags you look for?

I consider asking my clients to get tested for the above issues if there is difficulty with losing weight or maintaining weight loss. Or if there is fatigue or depression that has not been responsive to antidepressants.

If the thyroid is off, it impacts metabolism and can increase anxiety and depression. When people are under stress, they will tend to binge on carbs, such as chips, to calm down; then they go for something sugary to wake up. This cycle of eating poorly tends to keep insulin in an imbalance.

If we have been living in a high-stress situation and/or working too much for a long period of time, then adrenal hormones and cortisol may begin running amok. God did not intend for our adrenals to work at the levels that we expect them to. I envy many of the European ways, where they take a full month of "holiday" to give their bodies, souls, and minds time to heal and stabilize.

To ensure your stress hormones stay healthy, do the following:

1. Eat according to the Joy Diet in Appendix A.
2. Exercise daily.
3. Make love two to three times a week—in a marriage where there is plenty of mutual pleasure.
4. Enjoy a healthy spiritual relationship with God.
5. Stay connected to joy-producing family and friends.

6. I hear that melatonin lessens with age and can mean sleep is interrupted, which affects well-being. Do you recommend melatonin for sleep?

Yes, melatonin has many benefits, one of them being that it is highly effective for sleep. Taken along with GABA and magnesium in the evening, you may never reach for a Tylenol PM again! You'll get good sleep, pleasant dreams, and no "sleeping pill" fogginess the next morning.

7. Can I just supplement with progesterone cream from the health-food store? What is DHEA? Is it safe to experiment with over-the-counter supplements from health stores?

I know that many women have found relief from over-the-counter progesterone cream, and both men and women often swear by DHEA as a wonder supplement. However, it is easy with self-medication to quickly go over the optimal amount. So my suggestion would be to search out the best physician in your area who is a specialist in bioidentical hormone replacement. Get your hormones tested, and you will eliminate the guesswork. Also have follow-up tests every few months to make sure all is balanced.

8. When a woman comes into your office and complains of, say, low libido or agitation or anxiety or depression, how do you know whether she needs medication or supplements for these issues, or if it is most likely a hormone imbalance that is at the root of her issues?

The first question I would ask her is, "Has your libido or sexual satisfaction always been low, or is this recent?" I would also ask, "Is there a cyclical side to any of your issues? In other words, do you notice that you feel better or more passionate at some points during the month than others?"

I've seen women in a few cases experiencing all of the above issues, where balancing hormones alone does the trick. However, the majority of women I see need a combination of helps: better brain function after a peek at their SPECT scan or Amen Brain Test; a look at their nutrition, sleep habits, and hormones; and of course, a good look at the daily reality of the stress in their lives, including their relationships. I had one woman come into my office who had been on great medications and hormone replacement, ate well, and exercised—but none of that was enough to dampen the damage that her verbally abusive husband was inflicting on her daily.

There isn't enough nutrition or medication or supplements or hormones

NOTES

Chapter 1: This Is Your Brain in Love . . . or Is It on Drugs?
1. John Comwell, "Is Love Like a Drug?," *Sunday Times Online*, February 12, 2006, www.sensualism.com/love/druglove.html.

Chapter 2: Sexuality and Spirituality: Divine Balm for Your Soul and Brain
1. David Schnarch, *Constructing the Sexual Crucible* (New York: W. W. Norton & Co., 1991).
2. In fact, when it comes to practicing the healing art of marriage therapy I would say that the two men's works that have most influenced my practice are Dr. Schnarch's concept of the twin healing balms of sexuality and spirituality in a marriage and Dr. Daniel Amen's research on the brain and its practical application to relationship improvement. The third greatest influence has been my personal study of the Bible.
3. Information taken from Schmuley Boteach, *Kosher Sex: A Recipe for Passion and Intimacy* (New York: Double Day, 1999); www.aish.com.

Chapter 3: Bring Your Best Brain to the Marriage!
1. *Hebrew-Greek Key Study Bible*, New International Version (Chattanooga, TN: AMB Publishers, 1996), 1534.
2. John Gottman, *The Art and Science of Love* DVD Workshop for Couples. This DVD can be ordered from www.gottman.com. Excellent material, highly recommended.

Chapter 4: The Scattered Lover (Prefrontal Cortex)
1. Joseph McBride, *Steven Spielberg: A Biography* (New York: Da Capo Press, 1999), 40.
2. Fred A. Bernstein, *The Jewish Mothers' Hall of Fame* (New York: Doubleday, 1986), 2–3.
3. www.amenclinic.com.

Chapter 5: The Overfocused Lover (Cingulate Cyrus)
1. Daniel G. Amen, *Images of Human Behavior* (Newport Beach, CA: Mindworks Press, 2004), "Images of Obsessive Compulsive Spectrum Disorders," www.docamen.net/bp/atlas/ch13.php. Used by permission.

Chapter 6: The Blue Mood Lover (Deep Limic System)
1. Mark A. Whisman, "Psychopathology and Marital Satisfaction: The Importance of Evaluating Both Partners," *Journal of Consulting and Clinical Psychology* 72 (October 2004: 830–838.
2. Used by permission.
3. Tina Zahn with Wanda Dyson, *Why I Jumped* (Grand Rapids: Revell, 2006), 14.
4. Ibid.
5. Compiled from several sources, including Julia Ross, *The Mood Cure* (New York: Penguin, 2003); Daniel Amen, *Change Your Brain, Change Your Life* (New York: Three River Press, 1999); and Hyla Cass and Patrick Holford, *Natural Highs: Supplements, Nutrition, and Mind-Body Techniques to Help You Feel Good All the Time* (New York: Avery Trade, 2003).

6. Daniel Amen and Lisa C. Routh, *Healing Anxiety and Depression* (Berkley: Berkley Trade, 2004), 47–76.

7. www.marriage.about.com/od/entertainmen1/p/paulnewman.htm.

8. A thirty-year study at Duke University, reported in the 1982 journal *Gerontologist*, found that the frequency of sexual intercourse, for men, and the enjoyment of sex, for women, predicted longevity.

9. Ted McIlvenna, "Sexually Active People Draw Far More Joy," www.articlesbase .com/men's-health-articles/health-benefits-of-the-male-orgasm-835266.html.

10. Candis Hale, "The Benefits of Orgasm: Getting Hot and Healthy!" www.ezilon .com/articles/articles/4699/1/The-Benefits-of-Orgasm:-Getting-Hot-and-Healthy!, 4/12/2007.

11. www.streetdirectory.com/travel_guide/25236/health/health_benefits_of_the_male_ orgasm.html.

12. http://thinkexist.com/quotation/the_friend_who_can_be_silent_with_us_in_a_ moment/209085.html.

Chapter 7: The Agitated Lover (Temporal Lobes)

1. Information about Sinatra was gleaned and summarized from Anthony Summers and Robbyn Swan, *Sinatra: the Life* (New York: Alfred A. Knopf, 2005) and the Web site http://www.anecdotage.com/index.php?aid=11402.

2. Amen, *Change Your Brain, Change Your Life*, 189.

3. Susan Isaacs, *Angry Conversations with God: A Snarky but Authentic Spiritual Memoir* (Nashville, TN: FaithWords, 2009), 32.

4. Stephen Brookes, "Chant: A Healing Art," *Washington Times*, June 25, 2008.

5. Ibid.

6. Linda Dahlstrom,"Never to part: Devoted couples share life, death," www.msnbc .msn.com/id/26980587.

Chapter 8: The Anxious Lover (Basal Ganglia)

1. Gene Wilder, *Kiss Me Like a Stranger: My Search for Love and Art*, unabridged audio CD (New York: Macmillan Audio, 2005).

2. Susan Jeffers, *Feel the Fear and Do It Anyway* (New York: Harcourt Children's Books, 1987).

Chapter 9: The Secret to Lasting Love

1. Byron Katie, www.thework.com.

2. www.sciencedaily.com/releases/2008/01/080104122807.html.

3. Used by permission.

Appendix A: The Joy Diet

1. Alan C. Logan, *The Brain Diet* (Nashville: Cumberland House Publishing, 2007).

Appendix D: New Hope: Women and Hormones

1. Steven Hotze, *Hormones, Health, and Happiness* (New York: Wellness Central, 2007), 107.

D r. Earl Henslin has a doctorate in clinical psychology and is a licensed marriage and family therapist. He is a former part-time faculty member at the Rosemead Graduate School of Psychology at Biola University and author of six other books. He helped found Overcomers Outreach to aid churches in establishing support groups. In addition to clinical practice, Dr. Henslin stays busy leading seminars for professional counselors, business executives, and laypeople, helping them to become "brain healthy." He is also a diplomate to the American Academy of Experts in Traumatic Stress.

For the past fourteen years—working closely with brain imaging research pioneer Daniel G. Amen, MD—Dr. Henslin has been integrating brain imaging into the treatment of psychological, physical, and spiritual problems at his counseling practice, Henslin and Associates, a Christian counseling group in Brea, California.

- For speaking availability or speaking schedule
- To order other books and e-books by Dr. Henslin
- To sign up to receive the *Brain-Heart Matters Newsletter*

please visit us at

www.drhenslin.com

or call us at 714-256-2807

- To schedule a personal counseling appointment,

whether in person or by phone,

please go to

www.henslinandassoc.com

or contact us at 714-256-HOPE (714-256-4673)

Our offices are located in Brea, California.

For information about Amen Clinics or to see more SPECT images, please visit www.amenclinic.com. There are several Amen Clinics, but the one closest to our office is located in Newport Beach, California.